Microsoft

Leading AI Transformation: Strategy, Governance, and Security Considerations

by Yuri Diogenes

AF720477

Leading AI Transformation: Strategy, Governance, and Security Considerations

Published with the authorization of Microsoft Corporation by: Pearson Education, Inc.

Copyright © 2027 by Pearson Education, Inc.

Hoboken, New Jersey

All rights reserved. This publication is protected by copyright, and permission must be obtained from the publisher prior to any prohibited reproduction, storage in a retrieval system, or transmission in any form or by any means, electronic, mechanical, photocopying, recording, or likewise. For information regarding permissions, request forms, and the appropriate contacts within the Pearson Education Global Rights & Permissions Department, please visit *www.pearson.com/global-permission-granting.html.*

No patent liability is assumed with respect to the use of the information contained herein. Although every precaution has been taken in the preparation of this book, the publisher and author assume no responsibility for errors or omissions. Nor is any liability assumed for damages resulting from the use of the information contained herein. Please contact us with concerns about any potential bias at *https://www.pearson.com/report-bias.html.*

ISBN-13: 978-0-13-594135-5
ISBN-10: 0-13-594135-0

Library of Congress Control Number: 2026948738

1 2026

Trademarks

Microsoft and the trademarks listed at http://www.microsoft.com on the "Trademarks" webpage are trademarks of the Microsoft group of companies. All other marks are property of their respective owners.

Credits

The visual elements in this publication were created using ChatGPT by OpenAI, with prompts and creative direction provided by the author.

Warning and Disclaimer

Every effort has been made to make this book as complete and as accurate as possible, but no warranty or fitness is implied. The information provided is on an "as is" basis. The author, the publisher, and Microsoft Corporation shall have neither liability nor responsibility to any person or entity with respect to any loss or damages arising from the use of the information contained in this book or from the use of the programs accompanying it.

EDITOR-IN-CHIEF
Julie Phifer

EXECUTIVE EDITOR
Loretta Yates

ACQUISITIONS EDITOR
Shourav Bose

DEVELOPMENT EDITOR
Rick Kughen

MANAGING EDITOR
Sandra Schroeder

SENIOR PROJECT EDITOR
Tracey Croom

COPY EDITOR
Rick Kughen

INDEXER
Timothy Wright

PROOFREADER
Donna E. Mulder

TECHNICAL EDITOR
Dominik Hoefling

COVER ILLUSTRATION
putilov_denis/stock.adobe.com

COVER DESIGNER
Twist Creative, Seattle

COMPOSITOR
codeMantra

GRAPHICS
ChatGPT

Dedication

I dedicate this book to my mother, Maria Salete Mascarenhas Diogenes, who passed away in September 2025. Thank you for your unconditional love, your guidance, and the countless lessons you taught me throughout my life. I miss you every day, Mom.

Contents at a Glance

	Acknowledgments	ix
	About the author	xi
	Introduction	xiii
	Foreword	xvii
CHAPTER 1	Identify the business value of generative AI solutions	1
CHAPTER 2	Identify benefits, capabilities, and opportunities for Microsoft's AI apps and services	23
CHAPTER 3	Identify an implementation and adoption strategy for Microsoft's AI apps and services	49
CHAPTER 4	Design identity, data, and cloud security for AI solutions	71
APPENDIX A	Preparing for AI Transformation Leader Exam (AB-731)	97
	Index	105

Contents

Acknowledgments . . . . *ix*

About the author . . . . *xi*

Introduction . . . . *xiii*

Foreword . . . . *xvii*

Chapter 1 Identify the business value of generative AI solutions 1

Identify the foundational concepts of generative AI 1

Describe the differences between generative AI and other types of AI 2

Select a generative AI solution to meet business needs 4

Describe the differences between AI models, including fine-tuned and pretrained models 6

Explain the cost drivers in Gen AI usage, including tokens and return on investment (ROI) considerations 7

Identify the challenges of using generative AI solutions, including fabrications, reliability, and bias 9

Identify when generative AI solutions can provide business value, including scalability and automation 11

Identify the benefits and capabilities of generative AI solutions 13

Describe the impact of prompt engineering 13

Identify business requirements for grounding solutions 15

Understand how retrieval-augmented generation (RAG) is used for AI solutions 16

Understand the impact of data on AI solutions, including data type, data quality, and representative datasets 17

Identify scenarios when machine learning adds value. 19

Next steps 20

Chapter 2 Identify benefits, capabilities, and opportunities for Microsoft's AI apps and services 23

Identify the benefits and capabilities of Microsoft 365 Copilot and Microsoft Copilot 23

Map business processes and use-cases to Copilot 24

Understand differences in capabilities between versions of Copilot 26

Understand the capabilities of Microsoft 365 Copilot Chat web and mobile experiences 27

Understand capabilities of the Copilot experience in various Microsoft 365 apps 28

Understand the capabilities of Microsoft Copilot Studio 30

Understand the capabilities of Microsoft Graph 32

Identify the benefits and capabilities of an integrated Microsoft AI solution, including risk mitigation and safety benefits 33

Map business processes and use-cases to Microsoft's AI apps and services 35

Identify when to use Researcher or Analyst in Copilot 36

Identify when to build, buy, or extend, including the Microsoft 365 Copilot extensibility framework 38

Identify the benefits and capabilities of Microsoft Foundry services 39

Map business processes and use-cases to Microsoft Foundry services 40

Identify capabilities of Microsoft Foundry services, including Azure Vision in Foundry services, Azure AI Search, and Microsoft Foundry 41

Match an AI model to a business need 43

Identify the benefits of Microsoft Foundry services for generative AI, including scalability and security 44

Next steps 46

Chapter 3 Identify an implementation and adoption strategy for Microsoft's AI apps and services 49

Align an AI strategy with Microsoft's responsible AI policies 49

The importance of responsible AI 50

Establish governance principles for AI use 53

Establish an AI council to guide strategy, oversight, and cross-functional alignment 54

Plan for AI adoption across the organization 56

Establish an adoption team 56

Identify common barriers to adoption 58

Establish an AI Champions program 60

Understand Copilot license types, including pay-as-you-go, monthly, and included with a Microsoft 365 subscription 63

Understand Microsoft Foundry services subscription models, including pay-as-you-go and provisioned throughput unit (PTU) ... 66

Next steps 68

Chapter 4 Design identity, data, and cloud security for AI solutions 71

Designing considerations for Microsoft Entra as your identity security solution for AI 71

Everything starts with an identity 72

Identity signals as a foundation for Zero Trust and AI security 74

AI-powered identity protection and risk detection 75

Behavior-based user and sign-in risk scoring 77

Adaptive access with conditional access 77

Designing considerations for Microsoft Purview as your data protection solution for AI 79

Data security posture management (DSPM) for AI 79

Data classification and sensitive data detection in AI 81

Information protection for AI apps and agents 82

Data governance for AI 85

Designing considerations for Microsoft Defender for Cloud as your cloud security solution for AI 87

Risk prioritization and contextual security recommendations 88

Threat protection for AI workloads 90

Next steps 94

Appendix A Preparing for AI Transformation Leader Exam (AB-731) 97

Index *105*

Acknowledgments

I would like to thank Pearson/Microsoft Press for the almost two decades of partnership, and a special thanks to Shourav Bose and Loretta Yates. I would also like to thank my great friend and technical reviewer of this book, Dominik Hoefling, for the amazing work and constant feedback.

As you might have seen in the Foreword, the book started with a great contribution from David Weston. Thank you so much for your time, David.

Thank you to all my students, mentees, and everyone who attended my AI Security talks across the globe. Your feedback and insights helped me to shape this book!

–Yuri Diogenes

About the author

Yuri Diogenes has a PhD in cybersecurity leadership and a Master of Science in cybersecurity intelligence and forensics investigation. Yuri has been working at Microsoft since 2006, and currently, he is a principal PM manager at Microsoft CxE, where he manages the Defender for Cloud and Azure Network Security Teams. Yuri is also a Professor at the University of Texas at Dallas and EC-Council University. Yuri has published more than 30 books, mostly about information security and Microsoft technologies. Yuri also holds an MBA and many IT/Security industry certifications, such as CISSP, E|CND, E|CEH, E|CSA, E|CHFI, E|CTI, CompTIA Security+, CySA+, CASP, and MITRE ATT&CK Cyber Threat Intelligence. You can follow Yuri on X at @yuridiogenes and watch his Defender for Cloud in the Field show at aka.ms/MDCInTheField.

Introduction

AI is changing the way organizations think about work, leadership, security, and business transformation. But if you are like many leaders I talk to, you are probably not asking whether AI matters anymore. You are asking where to start, how to prioritize, how to avoid unnecessary risk, and how to turn all this innovation into measurable business value. That is the practical conversation this book is meant to have with you.

I wrote this book because AI adoption has moved beyond experimentation. Organizations are now expected to make real decisions about Microsoft 365 Copilot, Copilot Studio, Azure AI services, responsible AI, identity security, data protection, and cloud security. Those decisions are not only technical. They affect budgets, governance, productivity, trust, compliance, and culture. The goal of this book is to help you connect those pieces and build an AI strategy that is useful, secure, responsible, and aligned to the way your organization actually works.

Throughout the chapters, I will guide you through the concepts and decisions that matter most for AI transformation. We will start with the business value of generative AI, then look at Microsoft's AI apps and services, adoption strategy, responsible AI, and the security foundations required to protect identities, data, and cloud workloads. My intent is not to overwhelm you with theory, but to give you a clear way to think about AI in real business scenarios, including where it adds value, where it introduces risk, and where leadership must be intentional.

As you read this book, I encourage you to think about your own organization, your own users, and your own adoption journey. AI is not successful simply because it is deployed; it becomes successful when people trust it, use it effectively, and apply it to the right problems. My hope is that this book helps you move from AI curiosity to AI confidence, giving you the language, structure, and practical guidance needed to lead meaningful AI transformation with Microsoft technologies.

Who this book is for

This book is for decision-makers, architects, security leaders, and business stakeholders who are trying to make sense of AI beyond the hype. If you are responsible for shaping strategy, choosing the right Microsoft AI capabilities, securing data and identities, or helping your organization adopt AI in a practical way, this book was written with you in mind. You do not need to be a data scientist to benefit from it. Still, you should be willing to think about AI as both a business opportunity and a leadership responsibility.

Assumptions

This book assumes that you already have a working understanding of AI in a business context. You should be familiar with core AI concepts, the role of Microsoft 365 services in the modern workplace, and the kinds of capabilities Azure AI can bring to business solutions. I also assume you have some experience leading change, influencing technology adoption, or helping an organization move from strategy to execution.

How this book is organized

This book is organized as a practical journey through AI transformation, starting with the business value of generative AI and then moving into the Microsoft technologies, adoption practices, and security foundations that make AI successful in the real world. The chapters were written in a way that they build on one another, but I also want you to feel comfortable jumping into the section that matches the decision or challenge in front of you. If you are new to AI strategy, I recommend reading the chapters in order. If you are already working on a specific initiative, such as Copilot adoption, Azure AI solution design, or AI security, you can go directly to the chapter that helps you move that work forward.

The book is organized as described here:

- Chapter 1 introduces the business value of generative AI and explains the foundational concepts leaders need to understand before making investment decisions. It covers how generative AI differs from traditional AI, how to select the right type of AI solution for a business need, how models such as pretrained and fine-tuned models differ, and why cost, tokens, ROI, reliability, bias, hallucinations, prompt engineering, grounding, RAG, data quality, and machine learning all matter.
- Chapter 2 focuses on Microsoft's AI apps and services, including Microsoft 365 Copilot, Microsoft Copilot, Copilot Chat, Copilot Studio, Microsoft Graph, Azure AI services, Azure AI Search, Azure AI Vision, Azure AI Foundry, and the build, buy, or extend decisions leaders must make when mapping business processes to AI capabilities.
- Chapter 3 shifts from technology to adoption and governance. It explains how to align AI strategy with Microsoft Responsible AI principles, establish governance, create an AI council, build an adoption team, identify adoption barriers, launch

an AI Champions program, and make licensing and subscription decisions that support real usage and measurable value.

- Chapter 4 brings everything together through the lens of security, with practical design considerations for identity, data, and cloud protection in AI solutions. It covers Microsoft Entra for identity and agent security, Microsoft Purview for data protection, classification, governance, and DSPM for AI, and Microsoft Defender for Cloud for securing AI workloads across cloud and multicloud environments. My recommendation is to read this book as both a guide and a reference: follow it chapter by chapter if you want the full end-to-end story or return to specific chapters when you need help making a decision, explaining a concept, or designing a safer and more effective AI strategy.

- The appendix is included to assist you in preparing for the AI Transformation Leader Exam (AB-731).

While the goal of the book is broader than exam preparation, the structure intentionally follows many of the decisions and concepts an AI transformation leader must understand to identify business value, choose the right Microsoft AI capability, plan adoption, apply responsible AI principles, and design security controls for identity, data, and cloud environments.

If you are preparing for AB-731, use the chapters to build your understanding and use the appendix as a review guide to test whether you can explain the concepts in your own words. That is the real goal: not just passing an exam but also becoming confident enough to lead AI transformation responsibly.

Errata, updates, & book support

We've made every effort to ensure the accuracy of this book and its companion content You can access updates to this book—in the form of a list of submitted errata and their related corrections—at:

MicrosoftPressStore.com/AB731leadingAI/errata

If you discover an error that is not already listed, please submit it to us on the same page.

For additional book support and information, please visit *MicrosoftPressStore.com/Support*.

Please note that product support for Microsoft software and hardware is not offered through the previous addresses. For help with Microsoft software or hardware, go to *support.microsoft.com*.

Foreword

When Yuri asked me to write the foreword for his book on AI transformation, I thought long and hard about what my message should be. This is an important subject, and the stakes feel especially high right now.

Regardless of where you sit in the AI debate, one thing is clear: we are at an inflection point in technology. I've spent the last 20 years in cybersecurity, and today, I lead an AI security organization. From where I sit, this moment is both an opportunity and a risk. The good news is that we as leaders get to choose what we make of it.

AI is disrupting a wide range of industries, and security most of all. Attackers, as usual, are moving asymmetrically. They are quicker to put AI to work in their day-to-day operations. This doesn't mean some magic has been sprinkled over them and they've become unstoppable. Like the rest of us, they are simply raising their productivity. They augment skills they didn't have before, and they get more output from the skills they already have.

One reason attackers can do this faster than defenders is that they don't play by the rules. They have no governance. They don't have to lead an organization through change. They can focus on one thing: the outcome. I'm not suggesting we copy that minimalist approach, because it carries real risk. But it explains the gap, and it should worry us.

This book is for the people closing that gap, the ones leading through transformation across strategy, governance, and security. My message to you is simple: weigh the opportunity cost of not doing AI. Healthcare, manufacturing, agriculture, whatever your organization touches, the productivity gains on the table are enormous if we move fast enough to capture them.

The same holds for security. Every time we slow down in the name of caution, we pay an opportunity cost. When we refuse to lean into protecting our data and our identities, where AI can help so much, we pay again. Attackers are not waiting for us to get comfortable.

So, my ask is this: Put the skills in these pages to work—for your organization and for the broader good. Treat slowing down AI as the cost it really is. Yuri has laid out, clearly and practically, how to make this transformation, and I'd urge you to lean into it.

Use this book as your guidelines, and you'll be ready to drive the change. You'll be ready to build governance that sets real guardrails, the kind that lets you adopt AI quickly and in an agile way while keeping that opportunity cost low. And for the security professionals reading this, taking Yuri's advice to heart is how you keep attackers from getting ahead of you. Staying symmetric with them is better for all of us.

David Weston
Corporate Vice President, AI Security
Microsoft

CHAPTER 1

Identify the business value of generative AI solutions

"This is not about deploying another digital system. It's about rethinking end-to-end workflows."

Satya Nadella, Microsoft CEO

IN THIS CHAPTER, YOU WILL:

- Identify the foundational concepts of generative AI
- Identify the benefits and capabilities of generative AI solutions

Identify the foundational concepts of generative AI

Artificial intelligence (AI) has moved into the center of modern business strategy. What you see nowadays are organizations across different industries evaluating how AI can help them operate more efficiently. Business leaders are looking into AI as the transformational factor that will bring competitive advantage and direct gains from automating repetitive work, extracting insights from data, and creating entirely new digital experiences. While AI introduces extraordinary opportunities, accelerates decision-making, and enables new digital products and services, it also introduces significant governance responsibilities, including questions of transparency, accountability, and risk management.

Generative AI (Gen AI) has emerged as one of the most transformative technologies in recent years. Organizations are rapidly adopting Gen AI tools and developing Gen AI apps across different lines of business. Gen AI tools include conversational assistants, intelligent copilots, automated content creation platforms, and code generation systems. The adoption of these Gen AI tools within the business is pushing leaders to rethink how work gets done. What once required specialized expertise can now be accelerated through AI assistance. Tasks that previously took hours may now take minutes.

However, adopting Gen AI shouldn't be seen as the adoption of any other technology, as mentioned in Satya's quote at the beginning of this chapter; it is about rethinking the end-to-end workflow. Leaders must understand the business value, operational impact, governance requirements, and security considerations associated with AI systems. The organizations that succeed with AI transformation are those that treat AI as both a technical capability and a strategic initiative. For leaders, understanding

Gen AI is not about memorizing definitions; it's about recognizing where it fits within the broader AI landscape, how it creates value, and where it introduces risk.

It is important to acknowledge that AI is moving from simply assisting humans to increasingly acting on behalf of humans. This is where Agentic AI enters the conversation. Think of Agentic AI as AI that does not just respond to prompts, but also can pursue goals, make decisions within defined boundaries, orchestrate multiple steps, interact with systems, and adapt based on outcomes. Instead of asking AI to help you write an email, summarize a report, or generate a presentation, you might ask an AI agent to coordinate a customer onboarding process, investigate a security alert, reconcile financial discrepancies, or complete a workflow spanning multiple applications, with minimal human intervention.

The key difference is autonomy and action. Traditional generative AI applications are largely reactive: you ask, they answer. Copilots are more embedded and contextual, assisting you while you work inside familiar applications like email, productivity suites, or development environments. Agentic AI goes a step further. It introduces planning, memory, reasoning, tool usage, and the ability to take action toward an objective rather than simply generating output. In many ways, copilots are like highly intelligent assistants sitting beside you, while AI agents are more like delegated digital team members capable of executing assigned tasks. Of course, that added autonomy also introduces new leadership questions around governance, trust, identity, permissions, observability, and security. This is particularly important because, at the moment AI begins acting instead of merely advising, the organizational risk equation changes significantly.

Describe the differences between generative AI and other types of AI

I remember my first presentation about AI in about 2024; the audience was not aware that Gen AI was basically a broader evolution of artificial intelligence. To avoid the same misunderstanding, let's start with a *traditional AI* system. These systems are typically designed for prediction and classification tasks. For example, a fraud detection system evaluates transactions and flags suspicious behavior. A recommendation engine predicts what a user might want to watch next. These systems operate within defined boundaries and produce outputs based on patterns learned from historical data.

Gen AI is a class of artificial intelligence models capable of creating new content based on patterns learned from existing data. It can produce outputs such as text, images, code, audio, and even video. This differs from traditional analytical systems that primarily classify or predict outcomes. These models are typically based on deep learning architectures, particularly large neural networks trained on vast datasets. By learning relationships between words, images, or other data elements, generative models can produce responses that resemble human-created content.

But it is important to mention that the breakthrough in generative AI adoption largely came from large language models (LLMs). LLMs enabled AI systems to process context at scale. This made it possible for AI to understand instructions written in natural language and generate meaningful responses. Figure 1-1 has a representation of these components.

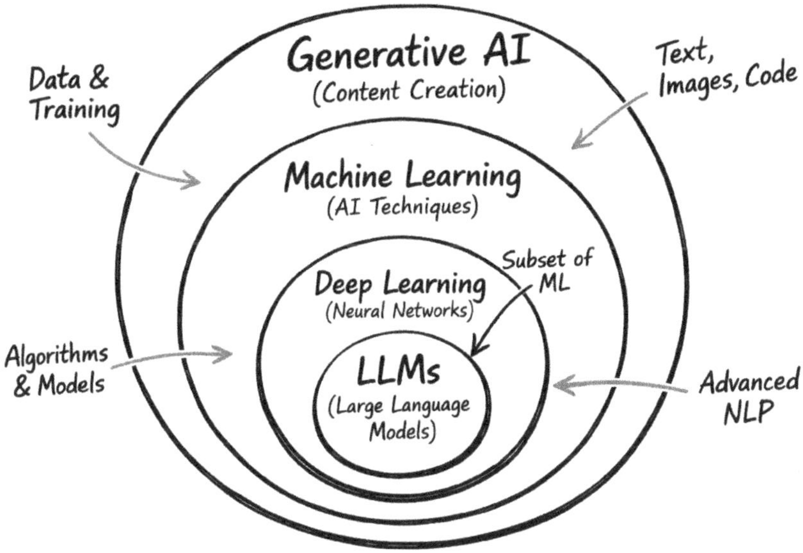

FIGURE 1-1 From LLM to Gen AI

Machine learning represents the broader discipline of algorithms that learn patterns from data to make predictions or decisions. Within machine learning is *deep learning*, a specialized subset that relies on multi-layered neural networks capable of identifying complex patterns in large datasets. Deep learning enabled the creation of large language models (LLMs), which are neural network models trained on large-scale datasets encompassing text, code, and multimodal content such as images and audio, to understand context, language structure, and semantic relationships. Natural language processing (NLP), represented in Figure 1-1 as the capability layer surrounding LLMs, refers to sophisticated natural language processing techniques that enable AI systems to understand context, semantics, intent, and linguistic nuances in human language. In this hierarchy, advanced NLP serves as the bridge that allows LLMs to transform learned language patterns into practical generative AI experiences such as text creation, code generation, and intelligent interactions.

Generative AI builds on these capabilities to generate new content (text, images, code, and other outputs) based on prompts provided by users. In summary, Gen AI is not a separate branch of AI but rather an application layer built on deep learning and machine learning technologies. Meanwhile, LLMs serve as one of the primary engines powering modern generative experiences. Table 1-1 has some important differences between traditional AI and Gen AI systems.

TABLE 1-1 Traditional and Generative AI Characteristics

Characteristic	Traditional	Generative
Interaction	Traditional AI often operates behind the scenes, embedded in systems.	Gen AI is frequently user-facing. Tools like Copilot and chat interfaces allow users to interact directly with AI systems using natural language. This changes the user experience dramatically, lowering the barrier to entry and expanding accessibility.
Determinism	Traditional AI systems often aim for consistent, repeatable outputs.	Gen AI systems are probabilistic. The same prompt may produce slightly different results each time, which can be both a strength (creativity, diversity) and a weakness (lack of consistency).

> **Important** From a business perspective, this distinction matters. Traditional AI optimizes processes while generative AI augments human capability.

Select a generative AI solution to meet business needs

Over the past few years, I've been talking to many chief information security officers (CISOs) about AI adoption. One question that usually comes up is: *Which Gen AI solution should I adopt?* My answer is always the same: Choosing the right Gen AI solution is not about adopting the most advanced model; it's about aligning capabilities with business objectives. The first step is to define the problem space clearly. If you are the AI leader, you should ask yourself: Is the organization trying to improve customer support? Automate document creation? Enhance developer productivity? Each of these scenarios maps to different types of Gen AI applications. Consider the following sample scenarios:

- The customer support team may benefit from conversational AI solutions integrated with knowledge bases.
- Software development teams may prioritize code-generation capabilities embedded within development environments.
- Marketing teams can focus on content generation tools that produce campaigns, social media posts, or product descriptions.

Once the use case is defined, organizations must evaluate whether to use prebuilt services, customizable platforms, or fully custom models. Prebuilt solutions, such as Microsoft Copilot experiences, offer rapid time to value with minimal setup. Platform-based approaches, like Microsoft Foundry, provide flexibility to tailor prompts, integrate data, and build custom workflows. As a business leader, you may want to go full customization, but fully custom models, while powerful, require significant investment and expertise.

Another critical consideration is data integration. Generative AI systems become significantly more valuable when grounded in organizational data. Techniques such as retrieval-augmented generation (RAG) allow models to access relevant documents and provide context-aware responses at query time, as shown in Figure 1-2. This process ensures the outputs are not only fluent but also accurate and aligned with business knowledge.

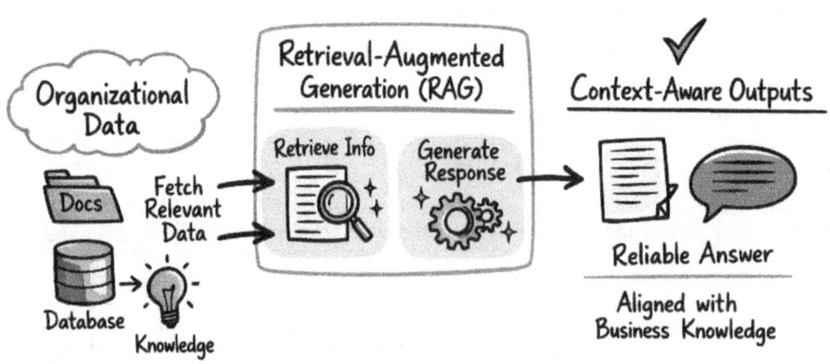

FIGURE 1-2 Data integration

Microsoft AI ecosystem has solutions for different needs according to the business scenario. Table 1-2 has some use case scenarios and how they map to the different Microsoft solutions.

TABLE 1-2 Mapping Business Scenarios with an AI Approach

Business scenario	Microsoft Solution	Rationale
Employees want help drafting emails, summarizing meetings, and creating documents inside the tools they already use.	Microsoft 365 Copilot	Microsoft 365 Copilot is embedded directly into Microsoft 365 apps, such as Outlook, Word, Teams, and Excel, minimizing change management and accelerating adoption. It delivers fast productivity gains without custom development.
A company needs a conversational AI assistant grounded in internal policies and procedures.	Copilot Studio + Microsoft 365 Copilot (grounded)	Copilot Studio allows organizations to build custom agents that use verified enterprise data. All that while still benefiting from Microsoft 365 Copilot's security and identity controls. This is preferred when responses must be accurate, explainable, and compliant.
Leaders want an AI solution that answers questions using internal documents that change frequently.	Microsoft Foundry (with RAG architecture)	RAG allows the model to retrieve up-to-date enterprise content at runtime instead of retraining models. This reduces hallucinations, lowers operational cost, and ensures current data usage.
A business wants to experiment with generative AI use cases before scaling organization-wide.	Microsoft Foundry	Microsoft Foundry supports experimentation, model selection, evaluation, and governance in a controlled environment. Microsoft Foundry is the preferable solution when the scenario includes exploration, prototyping, or future scalability rather than immediate end-user productivity.
Marketing teams need to generate product descriptions from structured specifications.	Azure OpenAI in Foundry Models	This is a classic content-generation scenario where Gen AI adds value by transforming structured inputs into natural language outputs. Microsoft Foundry provides flexibility and scale without forcing Copilot adoption where it may not fit existing workflows.
A customer support organization wants AI-generated responses, but must ensure Responsible AI principles.	Microsoft Copilot (with governance controls)	Microsoft Copilot integrates Responsible AI safeguards such as transparency, security, and identity controls. In scenarios like this, you should prioritize trust, inclusiveness, and accountability over raw capability.
A company needs AI to predict outcomes such as future sales demand.	Azure Machine Learning (not generative AI)	Predictive forecasting is a machine learning problem, not a generative AI use case.

Security and compliance also play a role in solution selection. Organizations must consider where data is processed, how it is stored, and whether the solution aligns with regulatory requirements. In Chapter 4, you will learn more about security considerations for AI. Ultimately, the best solution is one that balances capability, cost, scalability, and governance, while delivering measurable business outcomes.

Describe the differences between AI models, including fine-tuned and pretrained models

From the outside, you may think of Gen AI as an easy interactive interface to generate content, but in the heart of Gen AI are models, complex mathematical systems trained on vast amounts of data. Understanding the differences between model types is essential for making informed decisions.

Pretrained models are trained on large, diverse datasets and are designed to be general-purpose. They have already learned about the language structure, general facts, common reasoning patterns, and have broad knowledge across many domains. For this reason, these models can perform a wide range of tasks without additional training. For example, a pretrained language model can answer questions, summarize text, and generate content across multiple domains. The strength of pretrained models lies in their breadth. They provide a strong baseline and are often sufficient for many applications when combined with effective prompting and contextual grounding. Microsoft positions pretrained models as

- Fast to adopt
- Broadly capable
- Suitable for many business scenarios without customization

Fine-tuned models are adapted to specific tasks or domains. Fine-tuning involves training a pretrained model on a smaller, specialized dataset to improve performance in a particular context. The goal is to change how the model behaves, not what it retrieves. For example, a model can be fine-tuned on legal documents to better understand legal terminology and produce more accurate outputs in that domain.

Fine-tuning offers precision and specialization, but it comes with trade-offs. It requires labeled data, computational resources, and ongoing maintenance. Additionally, fine-tuned models may become less flexible outside their target domain. Below are some advantages and disadvantages of this model:

- Advantages
  - Higher accuracy for narrow use cases
  - More consistent outputs at scale
- Disadvantages
  - Higher cost (training + maintenance)
  - Requires quality, labeled data
  - Slower to adapt to change

In Figure 1-3, you can see a quick comparison between these two models based on use case scenarios.

From the leadership perspective, the decision is not just technical; it is strategic. Organizations must decide whether to invest in customization or leverage the flexibility of pretrained systems. Table 1-3 has some examples of when to use pretrained versus fine-tuned models.

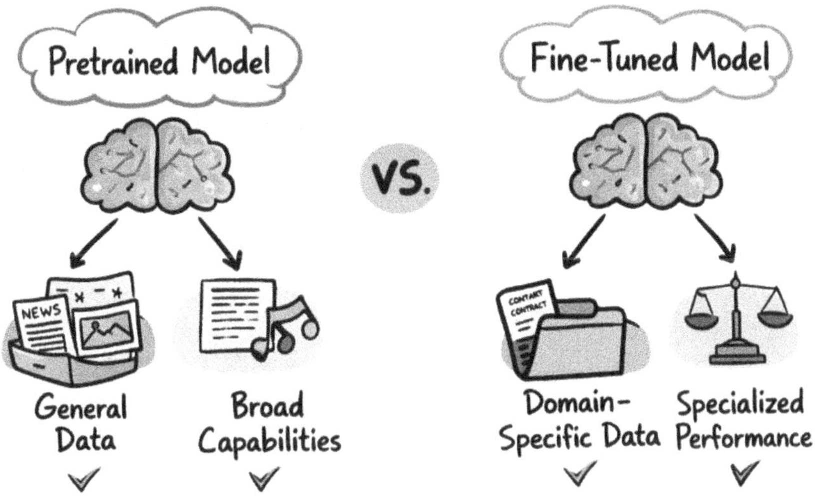

FIGURE 1-3 Comparison between models

TABLE 1-3 Pretrained versus Fine-Tuned Models

Model	Recommended Scenario
Pretrained	■ The use case is broad or exploratory ■ Speed matters more than precision ■ The organization is early in AI adoption ■ The required knowledge is relatively stable and well-represented in general training data
Fine-tuned	■ Output must be highly consistent ■ Domain language or format is critical ■ You have sufficient high-quality training data ■ The use case is stable and repeatable

Explain the cost drivers in Gen AI usage, including tokens and return on investment (ROI) considerations

Everyone wants AI until they start discussing the cost. This is what I've been hearing as I talk to many customers across the globe. The situation can get even worse when a lack of planning leads to high-scale enablement, followed by an astronomical bill that leads companies to question the entire AI adoption. For this reason, one of the most important aspects of Gen AI adoption is understanding cost. Unlike traditional software, where costs are often fixed or predictable, Gen AI introduces a consumption-based model. It is worth noting that Gen AI cost models vary significantly depending on the deployment approach. API-based access—such as Azure OpenAI via Microsoft Foundry—follows a consumption-based model where costs scale with usage. License-based products, such as Microsoft 365 Copilot, use a fixed per-user pricing model that is more predictable. Understanding which model applies to your deployment is essential for accurate budgeting.

This consumption-based mode introduces the concept of tokens.[1] Tokens represent units of text processed by the model. Both input (the prompt) and output (the generated response) are measured in tokens. Costs are typically calculated based on the number of tokens processed. This means that longer prompts and responses increase costs. For example, a system that processes large documents or generates detailed reports will consume more tokens than a simple question-and-answer interaction. Another example is shown in Figure 1-4.

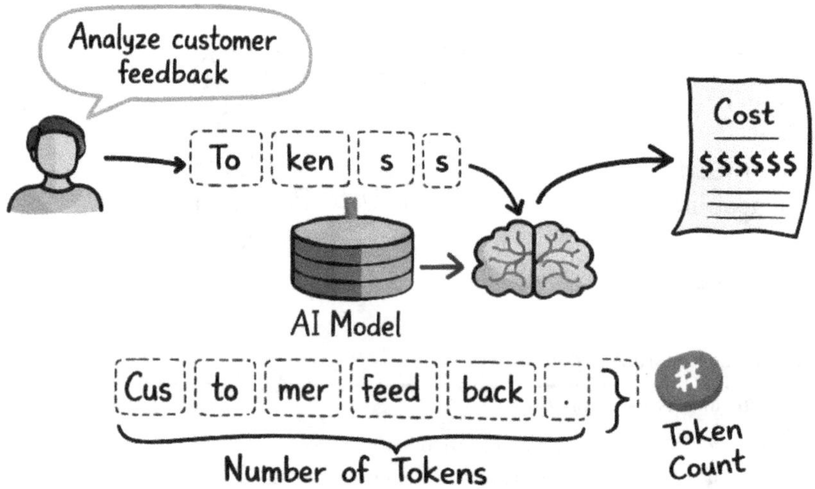

FIGURE 1-4 Use of tokens to calculate AI consumption costs

Uncontrolled prompts, excessive context, or verbose outputs can dramatically increase costs without improving outcomes. This means that more tokens don't mean more business value. In addition to that, there is another cost driver, which is the model selection. More advanced models generally provide higher-quality output but come at a higher cost. As a business leader, you must balance performance with budget constraints.

Although prompt engineering is often discussed as a quality topic, Microsoft also frames it as a cost control mechanism. On the one hand, a *prompt engineer* who is overly verbose on system prompts, injects large documents unnecessarily, and repeats instructions across prompts will increase the overall cost. On the other hand, a prompt engineer who writes clear, concise prompts, and uses RAG with relevant filtering for scope retrieval and standardized prompt templates will reduce costs. Effective cost management strategies include optimizing prompts, caching responses, using smaller models where appropriate, and monitoring usage patterns.

While those are the direct costs, there are also infrastructure and integration costs. Building a Gen AI solution often involves integrating with existing systems, managing data pipelines, and ensuring security and compliance. These costs can exceed the cost of model usage itself. As a business leader, the key question regarding ROI that you need to ask is not "how much does it cost?" but "what value does it create?" Gen AI can reduce operational costs, improve productivity, and enable new revenue streams.

[1] For more information about tokens, read *https://www.microsoft.com/en-us/microsoft-copilot/for-individuals/do-more-with-ai/general-ai/what-are-ai-tokens.*

For example, automating customer support can reduce staffing costs, while accelerating software development can shorten time-to-market. Also, you can use the following measures to evaluate ROI:

- Time saved per employee
- Reduction in repetitive manual work
- Faster decision-making
- Increased output consistency
- Ability to scale without proportional headcount growth

Let's use an example of Microsoft 365 Copilot generating meeting summaries for executives. The ROI justification can focus on the fact that it saves hours of executive time weekly, improves decision quality, and reduces follow-up meetings. While this scenario may have high token usage, it has even higher business value. According to Forrester's Total Economic Impact[2] study of Microsoft 365 Copilot, enterprises deploying Microsoft 365 Copilot can realize a projected 132–457 percent ROI over three years, with payback potentially occurring in less than six months, depending on adoption maturity and use case execution.

The analysis highlights that value creation extends well beyond individual productivity gains, with measurable business impact across revenue growth, operational efficiency, and workforce effectiveness, including an estimated 2.6 percent increase in top-line revenue through improved go-to-market execution, significant reductions in operating costs through automation and faster task completion, 25 percent faster onboarding for new employees, and nearly 20 percent lower attrition, driven by improved employee experience and reduced repetitive work. For enterprises, this positions Microsoft 365 Copilot not merely as a productivity assistant, but as a strategic AI investment capable of delivering meaningful financial returns while accelerating organizational transformation.

> **Important** ROI is not always immediate. Business leaders must consider long-term benefits, such as improved customer satisfaction, enhanced decision-making, and competitive differentiation.

Identify the challenges of using generative AI solutions, including fabrications, reliability, and bias

The Mata v. Avianca[3] case from 2023 is an example of when the citations included in the court cases generated by an AI system (ChatGPT) had many cited cases that did not exist; in other words, it was entirely fabricated by the AI. This is a classic fabrication (hallucination) that leads to reliability problems.

Fabrication, often referred to as *hallucination*, occurs when a model generates information that is incorrect or not grounded in reality. Because generative models are designed to produce coherent language, fabricated content can appear highly convincing. Keep in mind that fabrications represent a

2 Read more about this report at *https://tei.forrester.com/go/microsoft/M365Copilot/?lang=en-us*.

3 Read more about this case at *https://www.acc.com/resource-library/practical-lessons-attorney-ai-missteps-mata-v-avianca*.

business risk, not just a technical limitation, as incorrect outputs can damage credibility, lead to poor decisions, and create compliance or legal exposure. Business leaders must understand that fabrications are the expected behavior of Gen AI, so the correct leadership response is mitigation, not avoidance or denial. If you observe fabrications on your system, make sure to review some aspects that may lead to fabrications, such as

- The model lacks sufficient context
- The question goes beyond its training data
- Retrieved or grounding data is incomplete or outdated

Another concern is *reliability*. Gen AI systems may produce different outputs for the same input, making it difficult to ensure consistency. This can be problematic in scenarios where accuracy and repeatability are critical, such as legal or financial applications. In an enterprise environment, inconsistent outputs can reduce user confidence, slow adoption, and require additional human review. The opposite of human review is called *overreliance*, which is where users place too much trust in AI-generated output without verifying its accuracy, leading to poor decision-making. Make sure to update your security awareness training to educate all users about AI usage and how to avoid overreliance.

Another problem to be aware of is related to *bias*. Models trained on large datasets may inherit biases present in the data, which can lead to outputs that are unfair, discriminatory, or misaligned with organizational values. In 2026, Essex Police[4] paused the use of live facial recognition technology after a study done by University of Cambridge researchers revealed a systematic bias in how the AI identified people. This example is only one of many that clearly show that AI systems do not eliminate bias; instead, they can encode and scale it. As you plan your AI adoption, you should include the following practices to mitigate AI bias:

- Conduct bias testing and model audits
- Use diverse and representative datasets
- Implement responsible AI governance frameworks

> **Important** Bias is often discovered through evaluation, not by design. Systems initially appear to work, but deeper testing may reveal disparities.

Business leaders should be vigilant about these challenges because it affects trust in AI outputs, user adoption, brand reputation, and regulatory and compliance readiness. Microsoft defines these risks as leadership responsibilities and not engineering problems.

As you plan your AI adoption, make sure to include Microsoft Responsible AI to mitigate some of these scenarios. Microsoft explicitly includes fairness and inclusiveness as core *responsible AI principles*[5]

---

[4] Read more about this case at *https://www.theguardian.com/technology/2026/mar/19/essex-police-pause-facial-recognition-camera-use-study-racial-bias*.

[5] Read more about Microsoft Responsible AI at *https://www.microsoft.com/en-us/ai/responsible-ai*.

to address this challenge. In addition to responsible AI, organizations must include human oversight, validation mechanisms, and monitoring systems. Techniques such as grounding models in trusted data sources, implementing guardrails, and using evaluation metrics can improve reliability. Ultimately, the goal is not to eliminate risk entirely but to manage it effectively.

Identify when generative AI solutions can provide business value, including scalability and automation

I recall having a round table discussion with business leaders, where one of them said that he was receiving pressure from the CEO of the company to quickly start their AI adoption. The problem is that they really didn't know where to start and what value AI was going to bring to the company. Gen AI delivers the most value when applied to the right problems. Not every scenario requires generative capabilities, and misalignment can lead to wasted resources.

Microsoft frames generative AI value around two primary mechanisms:

- **Automation**—Doing existing work faster or with less human effort
- **Augmentation**—Helping people do higher-quality work at scale

When small time savings or quality improvements are multiplied across many users or interactions, you will see business value emerge. Another important use case is around scenarios that involve unstructured data. Traditional systems struggle with unstructured inputs like text, images, or audio. Generative models excel in these environments, enabling new use cases.

As mentioned before, automation is a major driver of value. Gen AI can automate tasks that were previously considered too complex for automation, such as writing reports, summarizing meetings, or generating code. This frees up human resources to focus on higher-value activities. For example, a customer support chatbot can respond to thousands of inquiries in parallel, something that would be impossible with human agents alone.

Rather than replacing humans, generative AI can enhance their capabilities through augmentation. For example, a security analyst can use AI to quickly analyze logs, generate reports, and identify patterns, improving both speed and accuracy. This is the classic scenario where Gen AI creates value by improving the quality of human output. For example, many managers in the organization are spending hours reviewing long documents. Gen AI can produce concise summaries and highlight key risks and decisions, which will allow managers to focus on judgment, not reading. This is augmentation, not replacement!

Review Table 1-4 to better understand Microsoft AI solutions and how they map to automation, scalability, and augmentation scenarios.

TABLE 1-4 Use case scenario values

Solution	Use Case Scenario	Automation	Scalability	Augmentation
Microsoft 365 Copilot	Employees need help drafting emails, summarizing meetings, and creating documents inside Outlook, Teams, and Word.	X	X	X
Microsoft 365 Copilot Chat	Executives want quick summaries and insights without switching tools or workflows.		X	X
Copilot Studio	The organization builds a custom internal HR or IT help desk assistant using company policies.	X	X	
Copilot Studio (Agents)	The business wants task-specific agents (e.g., onboarding, procurement requests) with defined workflows.	X	X	
Microsoft Foundry (with RAG architecture)	Employees ask questions over large, frequently changing internal document repositories.		X	X
Microsoft Foundry (Azure AI Search + Azure OpenAI)	Customer support teams need consistent, accurate answers grounded in product documentation.	X	X	
Microsoft Foundry	The organization experiments with multiple Gen AI use cases before standardizing and scaling.		X	
Azure OpenAI via Microsoft Foundry	The marketing team generates product descriptions from structured specifications.	X	X	
Microsoft Security Copilot	Security analysts investigate incidents and summarize complex attack data.		X	X
Azure Machine Learning (non Gen AI)	Business predicts future sales or demand using historical data.		X	

As you read this table, remember that

automation + scalability = cost reduction at scale

while

scalability + augmentation = productivity and decision quality at scale.

If you have all three—*automation*, *scalability*, and *augmentation*—then you have transformational ROI (which is the classic Copilot scenario).

Lastly, you should remember that value is not just about capability; it is about fit. Organizations must ensure that generative AI aligns with their workflows, culture, and strategic objectives. AI value depends on usage, not deployment. For example, 1,000 users saving 30 minutes a day creates more value than 10,000 users saving 2 minutes a day. In summary, low adoption means low ROI, while high adoption means exponential value.

Identify the benefits and capabilities of generative AI solutions

Now that you understand the foundational concepts of Gen AI, you are more equipped to identify the benefits and capabilities of Gen AI solutions. For leaders and practitioners, understanding Gen AI is less about the novelty of the technology and more about how it fits into business workflows. The real value of generative AI emerges when it is aligned with business goals, integrated with enterprise data, and governed responsibly. This section explores the core benefits and capabilities of generative AI, along with the practical considerations required to deploy it effectively in real-world scenarios.

Describe the impact of prompt engineering

Many people underestimate the importance of prompt engineering, not realizing that it has a direct impact on business because it helps to determine the effectiveness of Gen AI systems. Unlike traditional software, where behavior is defined by code, Gen AI systems are guided by instructions written in natural language. These instructions, known as prompts, shape how the model interprets a request and generates a response. The impact of prompt engineering can be dramatic. A vague or poorly structured prompt may produce generic or inaccurate results, while a well-crafted prompt can significantly improve relevance, accuracy, and usefulness.

For example, let's say you write this prompt: "Explain cybersecurity." This prompt will produce a broad and generic answer. In contrast, if you write a narrower question, such as "Explain the top three cybersecurity risks for a financial institution and suggest mitigation strategies aligned with NIST frameworks," it results in a much more targeted and valuable response. Prompt engineering also enables control over tone, format, and structure. Users can instruct models to respond as a technical expert, produce output in bullet points, or generate content suitable for executive audiences.

From a business perspective, prompt engineering allows organizations to extract more value from the same model without additional training or cost. This is why many enterprises invest in building prompt libraries and standardizing prompt patterns across teams.

Understand techniques of prompt engineering

You shouldn't think that effective prompt engineering is guesswork; it follows established techniques that improve output quality and consistency. One widely used technique is *role prompting*, where the model is assigned a specific role. For example: "You are a cybersecurity analyst reviewing incident logs." By using this technique, the model aligns its response with the expected perspective.

Contextual grounding within the prompt is another important technique. What this means is that you are providing background information, constraints, or examples that help the model to generate more accurate and relevant outputs. This is especially useful when dealing with domain-specific tasks. Providing the context by including *who*, *why*, and the *target audience* helps to get better results.

Few-shot prompting is another powerful technique. This technique is based on the premise that instead of asking a simple question, you provide examples of desired input-output. This guides the model toward the expected format and style. Below is an example:

Generate executive summaries in 2–3 sentences using the example below:

The company experienced a 20% increase in phishing attacks this quarter, mainly targeting finance employees.

Another technique is *chain-of-thought prompting*, which encourages the model to reason step by step, rather than jumping directly to an answer. This is especially useful for complex problems, decision-making, and analytical tasks. Here is an example of this prompt:

You are a cybersecurity analyst. Analyze the scenario step by step before giving the final answer.

Scenario:

A web application has an exposed admin panel accessible from the internet. It requires only a password (no MFA), and default credentials may still be enabled.

Think through this step by step:

1. Identify the risks
2. Assess likelihood of exploitation
3. Assess potential impact
4. Provide overall risk level

Another practical prompt engineering technique is output structuring, which means explicitly telling the AI how you want the response to be organized before it begins generating content. Large language models are remarkably capable, but without guidance, they may produce responses that are inconsistent, overly verbose, too generic, or formatted in ways that are difficult to use operationally. Output structuring reduces ambiguity by defining the expected shape of the answer. Think of it this way: if prompting is the act of asking a question, output structuring is specifying the format of the answer sheet. This becomes especially important in enterprise scenarios where AI outputs may feed directly into workflows, dashboards, automation pipelines, or decision-making processes.

For example, instead of asking "Analyze the cybersecurity risks of AI adoption," a better structured prompt would be: "Analyze the cybersecurity risks of AI adoption and present the output in four sections: Identity Risks, Data Protection Risks, Compliance Risks, and Operational Risks. For each section, include risk description, business impact, and recommended mitigation." The difference is significant because the second prompt produces something predictable and immediately actionable.

In addition to those techniques, you should also ensure that you add *constraints* when applicable. This means specifying what the model should not do, for example, "do not include assumptions not supported by the data." By simply adding this, you can reduce the likelihood of out-of-scope outputs.

Tip As your AI journey gets more mature, you should develop prompt templates for common use cases. These templates ensure consistency, reduce variability, and make it easier for users to interact effectively with AI systems.

Identify business requirements for grounding solutions

During my conversations with customers about AI adoption, one common misunderstanding is that AI will somehow inherently understand an organization's internal data. But it doesn't, and without grounding, the model relies on its pretrained knowledge. The problem is that this knowledge may be outdated, incomplete, or irrelevant to the specific business context. Grounding refers to the process of connecting AI outputs to trusted enterprise-specific data sources. Many business requirements trigger grounding, including:

- Regulatory or compliance needs
- Customer-facing accuracy
- Internal policy
- Legal guidance

Grounding ensures that responses are not only fluent but also accurate and aligned with organizational knowledge. Figure 1-5 shows the main elements required for grounding data in a business scenario.

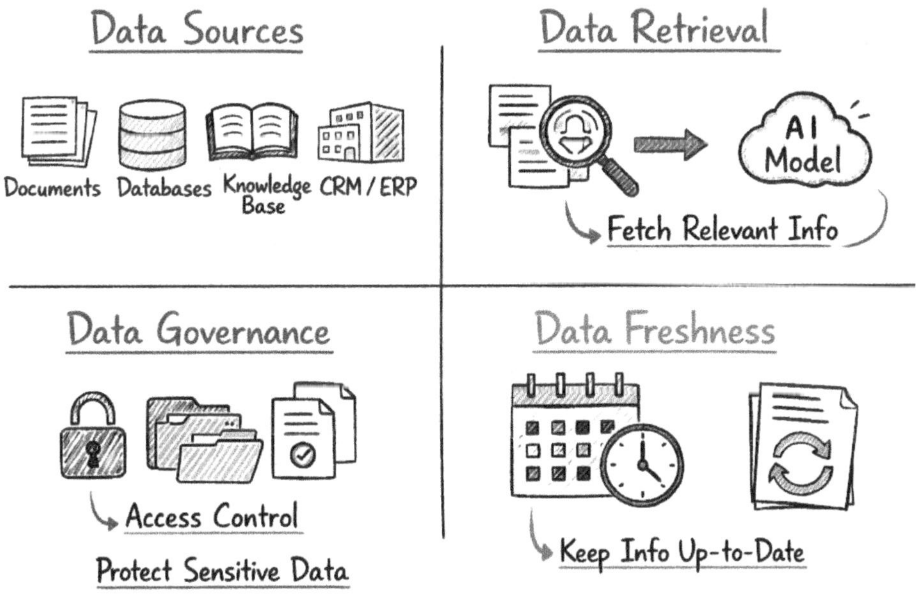

FIGURE 1-5 Grounding elements

As shown in Figure 1-5, there are four major elements in grounding:

- **Data sources.** These may include internal documents, databases, knowledge bases, or structured systems such as CRM or ERP platforms.

- **Data retrieval.** Also known as the process of retrieving and injecting relevant data into the model's context, this is typically achieved through retrieval systems that identify the most relevant information based on the user's query.
- **Data governance.** Here, the premise is that not all data should be accessible to all users (need to know principle). Grounding solutions must respect permissions and ensure that sensitive information is protected. But remember, data governance and protection must be in place before using the data for grounding. In Chapter 4, you will learn more about data protection for your AI journey.
- **Data freshness.** Ensure data freshness. Outdated information can lead to incorrect outputs, even if the system is technically functioning as expected.

Understand how retrieval-augmented generation (RAG) is used for AI solutions

A great follow-up to the topic of ground data is RAG, since it is one of the most effective techniques for grounding Gen AI systems. At a high level, RAG comprises two major components, as shown in Figure 1-6.

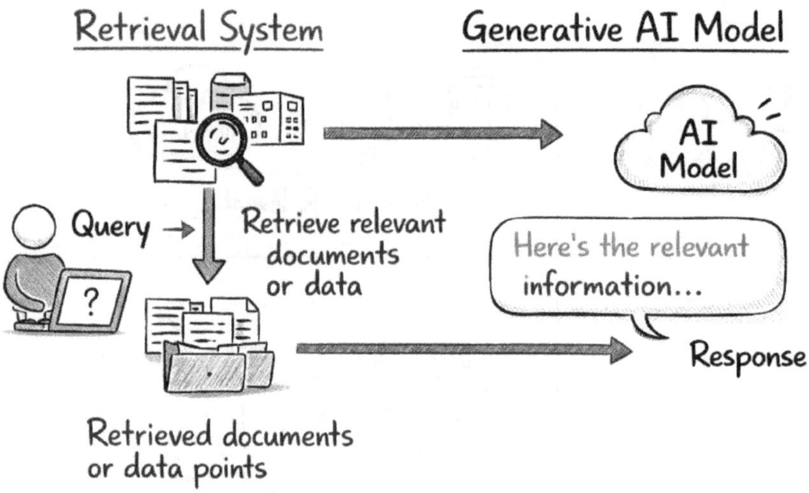

FIGURE 1-6 RAG components

The retrieval system searches for relevant information, while the generation model uses that information to produce a response. In other words, when a user submits a query, the system first retrieves relevant documents or data points. These are then passed to the model as part of the prompt, providing context for the response. The advantages of using RAG include

- **Accuracy improvement**: By grounding responses in real data, RAG reduces the likelihood of hallucinations.

- **Real-time knowledge integration**: Unlike pretrained models, which are static, RAG systems can access up-to-date information.
- **Scalability**: Organizations can integrate large volumes of data without retraining the model.

> **Important** Microsoft defines RAG as a three-step model (Retrieve, Augment, Generate): retrieves relevant content from a trusted data source, augments the user prompt with that content, and generates a response grounded in the retrieved information.

From a leadership perspective, you need to understand the use case scenarios in which RAG delivers value. One of these scenarios is the reduction of hallucinations. This is done by ensuring that answers are based on real documents and not probability alone. RAG also improves trust and adoption. This is important because users trust AI that reflects official sources. Another important aspect is the inherent support for governance, since access control can be enforced at retrieval time. Since there is no need to retrain every time content changes, RAG also lowers the long-term cost.

As a leader, you also need to educate the team that implementing RAG requires careful design. Retrieval quality is critical; if the system retrieves irrelevant or low-quality data, the output will be poor, which will affect trust and usability. In summary, RAG enables Gen AI to produce accurate, trustworthy, and up-to-date responses by grounding outputs in retrieved enterprise data rather than relying solely on model training.

Understand the impact of data on AI solutions, including data type, data quality, and representative datasets

In most of the AI projects that I've participated in over the last few years, I have mentioned the importance of data as the foundation of any AI system. Large organizations have many different types of data. The advantage of AI systems is that they can work with different types of data, including structured data (tables, databases) and unstructured data (text, images, audio).

Gen AI is particularly effective with unstructured data, which is often difficult for traditional systems to process. However, combining structured and unstructured data can unlock more powerful use cases. For example, combining customer transaction data with support tickets can provide deeper insights. While Gen AI excels with unstructured, language-heavy data, machine learning often performs better with structured, numerical data.

The quality, structure, and representativeness of data directly influence model performance and outcomes. This means that if the data is incomplete, outdated, biased, or poorly structured, AI outputs will reflect those weaknesses at scale. This is why data is treated as a business risk and governance concern, not just a technical dependency.

But what does data quality mean in this context? It means data missing values, duplicate records, outdated information, and inconsistent formatting. To ensure data quality, you need to enforce different types of processes such as validation, cleansing, and normalization. Another aspect of data quality is representative datasets. When the data does not reflect the diversity of real-world scenarios, the model may produce biased or unreliable outputs, which is something (bias) we covered earlier in this chapter. Use the list of questions below as you go through the rationalization of data quality:

- Is the data correct? (accuracy)
- Are key fields missing? (completeness)
- Is the data up-to-date? (freshness)
- Are definitions and formats aligned? (consistency)
- Is the data approved for use? (compliance)
- Is the data duplicated? (uniqueness)

> **Important** Microsoft positions data preparation as a prerequisite for high-quality AI experiences.

Microsoft emphasizes that data quality must contain three major elements, as shown in Figure 1-7.

FIGURE 1-7 Data quality llifecycle and continuous monitoring

The first stage (measured continuously) checks for the accuracy of incoming data, the completeness of required fields, the consistency of values and formats, and the alignment with expected distributions. The second stage (monitored for drift) checks the mismatch between the data used during training or initial setup and the data observed during production usage. Keep in mind that drift is expected to happen when some circumstances happen, for example, when user behavior changes, markets evolve, regulations shift, or when upstream systems change how data is collected. The last stage (updated as business context changes) is self-explanatory, but it basically includes anything that leads to updates in business, such as organizational restructuring, changes in customer expectations, or policy changes.

> **Important** Microsoft's Responsible AI guidance explicitly connects context changes to the need for data updates, not just model updates.

Identify scenarios when machine learning adds value

Does every single solution require a Gen AI application? Even so, there is hype that may lead you to believe that you need to be skeptical and cautious before leading your team to adopt AI for a project that doesn't need AI. While Gen AI is powerful, it is not always the right solution. In many cases, traditional machine learning approaches are more appropriate. For example, in cybersecurity, machine learning is often used to detect anomalies in network traffic. Gen AI, on the other hand, may be used to summarize incidents or assist analysts. Use Table 1-5 to identify where machine learning adds value:

TABLE 1-5 Scenarios where machine learning adds value

Task	Scenario
Prediction	Forecast demanding
Classification	Spam detection
Anomaly detection	Fraud detection
Optimization	Supply chain efficiency

> **Important** The rule of thumb is to match the tool to the problem. Gen AI excels at content creation and interaction, while machine learning excels at pattern recognition and prediction.

Describe the lifecycle of a machine learning solution

A machine learning solution follows a structured lifecycle, similar to software development but with additional considerations for data and models. The high-level lifecycle of a machine learning solution is shown in Figure 1-8.

Following is the machine learning lifecycle:

1. **Problem Definition.** Define the business problem and success criteria.
2. **Data Collection and Preparation.** Gather and prepare data for training, including cleaning and transformation.
3. **Model Development.** Select the algorithms, training models, and tuning parameters.
4. **Evaluation.** Assess model performance using metrics such as accuracy, precision, and recall.

5. **Deployment.** Once the evaluation results are in and everything is acceptable, integrate the model into production systems.

6. **Monitoring and Maintenance.** Continue monitoring for performance and updating the model as needed. Monitoring is considered a critical step for trust and accuracy.

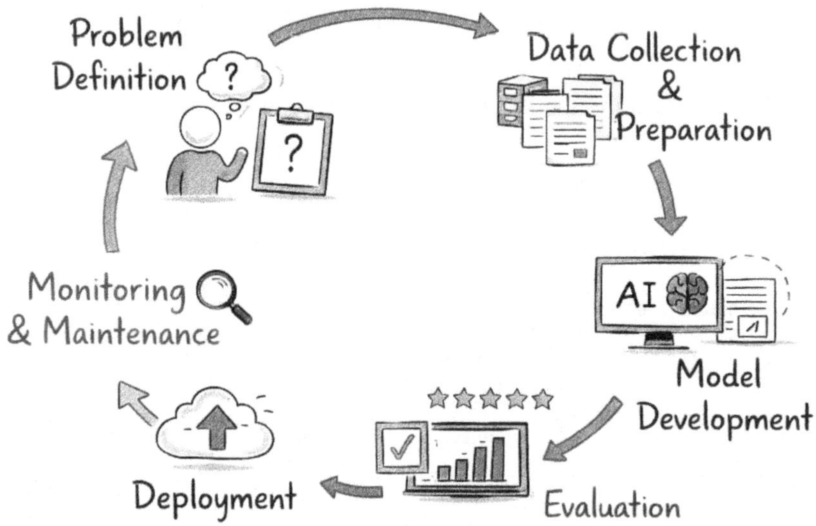

FIGURE 1-8 Machine learning lifecycle

> **Important** There are many aspects related to the importance of securing AI systems, including identifying security considerations for AI systems, application security, data security, and authentication requirements. All these aspects will be covered in Chapter 4.

Next steps

In this chapter, we discussed the foundational concepts of generative AI and the benefits and capabilities of generative AI solutions, including:

- Understanding the differences between generative AI and other types of AI
- Selecting a generative AI solution to meet a business need and describing the differences between AI models, including fine-tuned and pretrained models
- Explaining the cost of drivers in generative AI usage, including tokens and return-on-investment (ROI) considerations
- Identifying the challenges of using generative AI solutions, including fabrications, reliability, and bias

- Identifying how generative AI solutions can provide business value, including scalability and automation
- Describing the impact of prompt engineering and understanding the techniques that should be used to improve prompt engineering
- Identifying business requirements for grounding solutions and understanding how retrieval-augmented generation (RAG) is used for AI solutions
- Understanding the impact of data on AI solutions, including data type, data quality, and representative datasets
- Identifying scenarios when machine learning adds value and the machine learning lifecycle

CHAPTER 2

Identify benefits, capabilities, and opportunities for Microsoft's AI apps and services

"AI will create new industries and transform existing ones."

Jensen Huang, NVIDIA CEO

IN THIS CHAPTER, YOU WILL:

- Identify the benefits and capabilities of Microsoft 365 Copilot and Microsoft Copilot
- Identify the benefits and capabilities of Azure AI services

Identify the benefits and capabilities of Microsoft 365 Copilot and Microsoft Copilot

If you take a step back and look across your organization at how some of the work gets done today, you can clearly identify areas that AI can help. Not only from the perspective of automating manual tasks, but also intelligently consuming insights that will help you make faster decisions. Microsoft 365 Copilot and Microsoft Copilot are not trying to change what your organization does; instead, they are changing how your organization does it and how effective your decisions can be as an AI Leader. The intent is not to hand over to your employees another tool for them to learn, but to embed AI directly into the application that they already use in their everyday work. In this case, the scope of applications is Word, Excel, Outlook, PowerPoint, and Teams. The goal is to remove friction and speed up adoption, which can help you as an AI Leader to start seeing value almost immediately, without having to rethink your organization's entire way of working.

Microsoft 365 Copilot understands your employee's work and provides tailored answers based on the context of the user, which means that when they ask Copilot for help, it's not responding in a vacuum. The answers will be grounded on emails, files, meetings, and chats, and they will be bounded since they will focus only on the ones the user is allowed to see. That context comes from Microsoft Graph,[1] and it's what makes Copilot feel far more relevant than a generic AI chatbot. As a result, your

1 For more information about Microsoft Graph, visit *https://learn.microsoft.com/en-us/graph/overview*.

users will get an AI that's tailored to their response based on their profile, aligned to their role, and respectful of your organization's security and compliance boundaries.

Microsoft Copilot chat, on the other hand, builds on that idea by making AI available wherever your users are. The goal is to empower every user with an intelligent assistant in their workflow, whether they are preparing for a meeting, catching up after time away, or trying to get a quick answer without digging through documents. For organizations, that means AI becomes something people use naturally, not something reserved for power users or specialized teams.

From a leadership perspective, the key is not just understanding what Copilot can do, but also recognizing how it reshapes productivity, decision-making, and even organizational culture. Copilot acts as an augmentation layer, enhancing human capability rather than replacing it. This distinction is important, especially when communicating AI strategy at the executive level.

Map business processes and use cases to Copilot

To start mapping business processes and use cases to Copilot, you can start by asking a simple question: *Where are people spending time on repetitive, cognitive-heavy tasks?* Leadership will need to have this reflection exercise with their leadership team (LT) and managers to understand the business processes that can be improved with Copilot. Let's use as an example the scenario from the Finance department of an organization. Copilot can assist with summarizing financial reports, generating forecasts, and answering natural language questions over structured data. In another scenario, now with Human Resources (HR), Microsoft Copilot can help draft job descriptions, summarize candidate interviews, and generate onboarding materials. What becomes clear very quickly is that Copilot is not a single-use case tool; it is a horizontal capability that spans multiple functions.

Leadership must understand that when they are mapping business processes to Copilot, the goal isn't to sprinkle AI everywhere (which, unfortunately, many leaders are doing during this new wave of AI adoption). Instead, leaders must be intentional about where AI can remove friction in everyday work. As your leadership team reviews the organization's business processes, they may conclude that most business processes aren't broken; they are just weighed down by repetitive and time-consuming steps. That's where Copilot adds value by fitting naturally into how work already happens. Instead of redesigning processes from scratch, you're augmenting them, so people spend less time on busywork and more time on decision-making and outcomes.

Another important part of this mapping exercise is recognizing scale. In Chapter 1, you learned that *automation + scalability = cost reduction at scale*, while *scalability + augmentation = productivity and decision quality at scale*, and if you have all three, then you have transformational ROI (which is the classic Copilot scenario). Copilot delivers the most impact when a task is performed frequently by many people. If a process involves hundreds or thousands of employees writing emails, producing reports, analyzing spreadsheets, or attending meetings, even small-time savings compound quickly. That's why Copilot is often the right fit for organization-wide processes like communications, reporting, planning, and collaboration. When mapping use cases, leaders should always ask: *How often does this task occur, and how many people do it?*

Lastly, mapping business processes to Copilot helps avoid one of the most common AI pitfalls: over-engineering. You must realize that not every use case requires a custom AI solution or a new application. In many cases, Copilot already provides the capability out of the box, securely, compliantly, and within familiar tools. A practical approach is to map business processes into three categories, as shown in Figure 2-1.

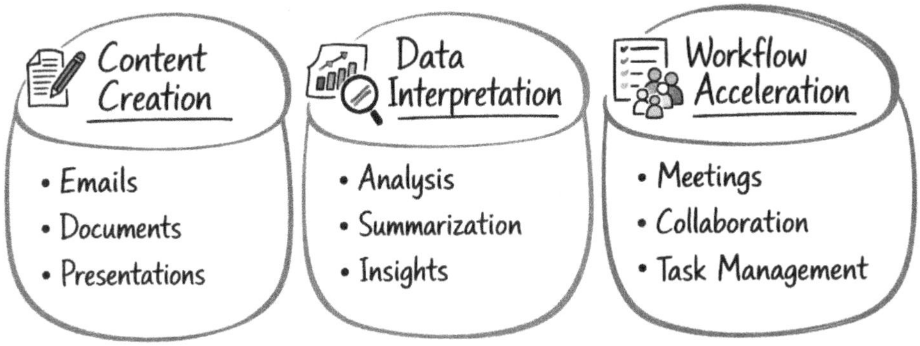

FIGURE 2-1 Mapping business processes

While Figure 2-1 offers some examples for each category, you should use this opportunity to revisit your business process and see which additional elements can be mapped to each category. Once mapped, leaders can prioritize use cases based on impact and ease of adoption. High-frequency, low-risk tasks are usually the best starting point.

> **Important** From the leadership perspective, keep in mind that you don't need to solve everything on day one. Start with common, low-risk use cases, prove value through daily usage, and then expand as people get comfortable.

A good mental shift here is to stop thinking in terms of "process automation" and start thinking in terms of "work support." Copilot isn't trying to take over full processes from end-to-end. Instead, the goal is to help with messy, manual parts inside those processes, the parts that slow your team down or break their focus. This leads to more productivity and more time to focus on more strategic projects.

As the AI transformational leader, you should think about change management and workforce enablement. The key question is not *"Will people use Copilot?"* but *"Will they use it effectively?"* At the same time, expectations must be set clearly. Copilot is a co-pilot, not an autopilot. Organizations that invest in skills, governance, and feedback loops will not only drive adoption but also ensure that the technology delivers meaningful, sustained business value.

Understand differences in capabilities between versions of Copilot

You have probably heard the word "Copilot" many times and wondered if this is a single product. In reality, Microsoft offers multiple Copilot experiences, each designed for a different scope and level of integration. Copilot is a family of experiences; each is designed for a different context and audience. Microsoft did this on purpose. Not every scenario needs deep access to organizational data, and not every user needs AI embedded inside enterprise workflows. Understanding these differences helps you avoid over-engineering and pick the version that delivers value with the least friction.

At a high level, the biggest distinction comes down to what data Copilot is grounded in. This is a fundamental point because some Copilot experiences work primarily with public web data, while others are deeply connected to Microsoft 365 data through Microsoft Graph. This difference directly affects relevance, trust, and compliance. When you are mapping business processes to Copilot use cases, this is also something you need to take into consideration. In other words, if the scenario requires AI responses that understand internal documents, meetings, and emails while honoring existing permissions, then Microsoft 365 Copilot is the right fit. On the other hand, if the scenario is more about general knowledge or light assistance, a simpler Copilot experience may be enough.

Another important difference lies in where (user experience) Copilot shows up. Some Copilot versions are embedded in apps like Word, Excel, Outlook, and Teams, while others show up as standalone chat experiences on the web or mobile. From an adoption perspective, this matters because when Copilot is embedded directly into the flow of work, it feels like a natural extension of what people already do. But when it's separate, it feels more exploratory or ad-hoc rather than deeply workflow-driven. There is value in both; it really depends on which experience you need to provide for the specific scenario to which you are mapping.

Leaders who are helping in the AI transformation also have a budget to honor, which in this case is important since there are different licensing aspects when adopting Copilot. Microsoft 365 Copilot is licensed as an add-on because it unlocks organization-wide productivity value tied to enterprise data and governance. Other Copilot experiences are included or freely accessible because they're meant to lower the barrier to entry and encourage experimentation. Table 2-1 has a comparison of Copilot versions:

TABLE 2-1 Practice mapping business scenarios with an AI approach

Copilot Version	Common Use Case Scenario	Main Features	How It's Licensed*
Microsoft Copilot (consumer/web)	General questions, learning, brainstorming, and everyday AI assistance	Web-grounded AI chat, image generation, and general Q&A, with no organizational context	Free or consumer subscription (not tied to Microsoft 365 tenant)
Microsoft 365 Copilot Chat (web and mobile)	Secure AI chat for work scenarios without deep in-app integration	Web-grounded chat, enterprise data protection, file upload, Copilot Pages, and IT controls	Included with Microsoft 365 subscription (no add-on license)

Copilot Version	Common Use Case Scenario	Main Features	How It's Licensed*
Microsoft 365 Copilot	Productivity and knowledge work inside Microsoft 365 apps	In-app Copilot for Word, Excel, Outlook, Teams, Loop, White-board, OneNote, Forms, and PowerPoint; Graph grounding; meeting summaries; document drafting	Paid add-on license for Microsoft 365 users
Microsoft Copilot Studio	Custom conversational agents and workflow extensions	Build and customize Copilot agents, connect to data sources, and enable low/no-code extensibility	Licensed separately; consumed as an exten-sibility platform
Microsoft Security Copilot	Security operations and incident response	Security-specific AI grounded in Microsoft Security ecosystems, and security data	Separate, role-specific (not Microsoft 365 Copilot)

* *The license column has information from March 2026. Make sure to visit https://www.microsoft.com/en-us/microsoft-365-copilot/pricing-new.*

Based on Table 2-1, it is possible to conclude that the key difference lies in context awareness. The more integrated Copilot is with organizational data and workflows, the more relevant and actionable its output becomes. So, as you choose the most appropriate Copilot for your scenario, take this deep integration into consideration when selecting the appropriate version.

Ultimately, the value of Microsoft 365 Copilot and Microsoft Copilot lies not just in what they can do today, but also in the foundation that they create for continuous innovation. By integrating AI into everyday work, aligning it with enterprise data and security, Copilot enables organizations to gradually unlock new capabilities and improve outcomes.

Understand the capabilities of Microsoft 365 Copilot Chat web and mobile experiences

Microsoft 365 Copilot Chat introduces a unified conversational interface that works across web and mobile platforms. This experience is particularly important because it becomes the "entry point" for many users interacting with AI. You can think of Microsoft 365 Copilot Chat as a secure, enterprise-ready AI assistant that helps you quickly gather information, summarize content, and draft ideas. You can upload files, ask follow-up questions, and save conversations into Copilot Pages.

It is important to emphasize that without a Microsoft 365 Copilot license, Copilot Chat is grounded mainly in web data, but still benefits from enterprise protections like identity, data boundaries, and IT controls. With a Copilot license, that same chat experience can be enriched with your work context (emails, files, and Teams meetings) based on your permission level. Figure 2-2 shows an example of the web interface that appears when you access Microsoft 365 Copilot Chat Web using the URL *https://m365.cloud.microsoft/chat.*

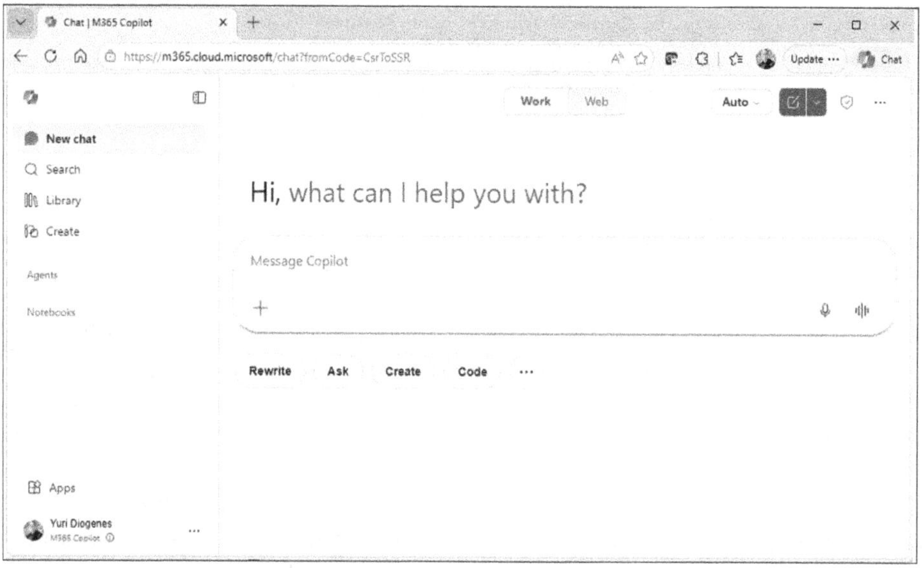

FIGURE 2-2 Microsoft 365 Copilot Chat Web

On this page, users can interact and ask questions such as: "Summarize the last three meetings I had with the security team and highlight action items." Microsoft 365 Copilot Chat doesn't just retrieve data; it synthesizes it. From a leadership standpoint, this reduces friction in knowledge access. Employees spend less time searching and more time acting.

> **Important** While Microsoft 365 Copilot Chat for work is an enterprise-safe AI experience, the consumer Copilot accessible via URL copilot.microsoft.com is designed for personal use. It relies on public web data and runs outside your organization's Microsoft 365 tenant.

Understand capabilities of the Copilot experience in various Microsoft 365 apps

One of the easiest ways to understand Copilot is to stop thinking of it as "one AI" and start thinking of it as many small helpers, each tailored to the application that you are already using to perform your daily tasks. These helpers will have peculiar behavior; in other words, Copilot behaves differently in Word than it does in Excel, and differently again in Outlook or Teams. This is intentional, and it is a good thing! Microsoft designed Copilot to adapt to the context of each application, so it helps with that specific kind of work instead of forcing a one-size-fits-all experience. Figure 2-3 shows a basic architecture[2] diagram of how this integration works:

[2] For a more in-depth explanation on the architecture and security boundaries, visit *https://learn.microsoft.com/en-us/copilot/microsoft-365/microsoft-365-copilot-architecture*.

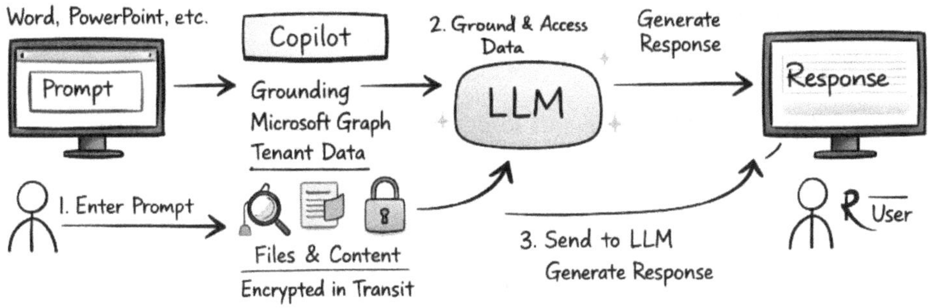

FIGURE 2-3 Microsoft 365 Copilot Chat Web

When a user, utilizing a Microsoft 365 application like Word or PowerPoint, enters a prompt in Copilot (1), Copilot preprocesses the input prompt by using grounding and accesses Microsoft Graph in the user's tenant (2). Based on this tailored request using grounding data, Copilot sends the grounded prompt to the LLM, which uses the prompt to generate a contextualized response for the user. That's when Copilot returns the response through the user interface (UI) of the application to the user (3).

Important Microsoft 365 Copilot uses Microsoft Graph to ground prompts in user-permitted organizational data and sends that context to Microsoft-hosted Azure OpenAI models, all within the Microsoft 365 tenant boundary and existing security controls.

In applications like Word and PowerPoint, Copilot is focused on creation and refinement. It helps you get past the blank page by generating first drafts, restructuring content, adjusting tone, or turning long documents into concise summaries. This is especially useful when you know what you want to say but don't want to spend time figuring out how to say it. In Excel, Copilot helps explain what your data is telling you, spot trends, create visualizations, and even suggest formulas. This enables information workers to be less occupied in wrestling with spreadsheets, quickly ask questions in plain language, and focus on making decisions based on the insights that come back.

In Outlook and Teams, Copilot helps to save time by summarizing long email threads, drafting responses, pulling out action items, and in the case of Teams, helps you to catch up on meetings you missed. Also in Teams, Copilot helps you stay oriented by recapping discussions, highlighting decisions, and outlining next steps. Leadership must understand that the value here is not only speed but also reducing cognitive load. Your team will spend less time catching up and more time contributing where it matters. Below is a quick summary of the main capabilities per application:

- **Word**: Helps draft, rewrite, and summarize documents
- **Excel**: Assists with data analysis, trend identification, and formula generation
- **PowerPoint**: Helps generate entire presentations from prompts or documents
- **Outlook**: Helps draft emails and summarizes threads

- **Teams**: Captures meeting notes, decisions, and action items in real time
- **Loop**: Helps with collaborative content creation
- **Whiteboard**: Helps draft natural language ideas into themes
- **OneNote**: Helps draft plans and generate ideas
- **Forms**: Helps draft questionnaires, surveys, and other form-based ideas

Bearing in mind those capabilities and use case scenarios are important, but as the AI transformational leader, you need to plan Microsoft 365 Copilot adoption by first establishing clarity of purpose. This should not be seen as just a technology rollout; it's a productivity transformation. As a Leader, you should ask: *Where do we lose the most time today? Which roles are overloaded with repetitive work? What outcomes do we want to accelerate? Decision-making, content creation, or data analysis?* The organizations that see the most value are the ones that tie Copilot usage directly to business scenarios, not generic enablement, for example, reducing executive reporting cycles, accelerating proposal creation, or improving meeting follow-ups. Without this alignment, Copilot risks becoming an interesting tool rather than a measurable driver of impact.

Understand the capabilities of Microsoft Copilot Studio

In Table 2-1, you learned that Microsoft Copilot Studio[3] has a different use case scenario when compared with Microsoft Copilot. If Microsoft 365 Copilot is the AI that helps you work better, Microsoft Copilot Studio is the tool that lets your organization teach AI how your business works. Microsoft Copilot Studio is where you go when the built-in Copilot features aren't quite specific enough, and you want something more tailored. Think of Copilot Studio as the place where Copilot becomes customizable without forcing you into a heavy development lifecycle or complex AI engineering.

You can also think about Copilot Studio's main mission to build AI Agents,[4] which are AI assistants that can answer questions, guide users, and take actions based on your instructions and data. The good news is that you don't need to be a developer or data scientist to do this. The experience is low-code and visual, which means business teams can design how these agents behave, what information they use, and how they interact with users. That's a huge shift from the old days of chatbots that required weeks of scripting and testing. For example, a company can use Copilot Studio to build an Agent that interacts with internal ticketing systems, retrieves policy documents, or automates approval workflows. Agents created in Copilot Studio can use enterprise data sources, including SharePoint, OneDrive, and approved websites. This ensures that responses are grounded in trusted content rather than generic web results. You can also extend these agents with Power Platform connectors and custom APIs, as shown in Figure 2-4.

---

[3] For more information about Microsoft Copilot Studio pricing, visit *https://www.microsoft.com/en-us/microsoft-365-copilot/pricing/copilot-studio.*

[4] For more information about AI Agents, read *https://news.microsoft.com/source/features/ai/ai-agents-what-they-are-and-how-theyll-change-the-way-we-work/.*

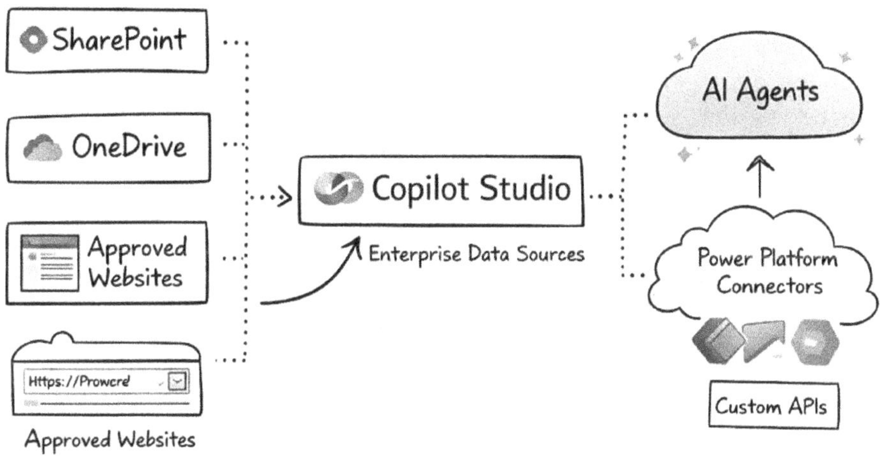

FIGURE 2-4 Agents created in Copilot Studio

It is also valid to say that Leaders usually don't start their AI journey by encouraging teams to build agents using Microsoft Copilot Studio. First, they learn how people use Microsoft 365 Copilot and Copilot Chat, where friction exists, and where generic AI stops being enough. Copilot Studio comes into play once you've identified repeatable patterns, questions people keep asking, tasks that keep getting handed off, or processes that always require manual intervention. In other words, you don't adopt Copilot Studio because it's powerful; you adopt it because you've already seen where power is needed. Having said that, each business has different needs according to its maturity level, and in some cases, some businesses may need to start their journey by creating custom agents based on pre-determined scenarios that they feel cannot be solved only by using Microsoft 365 Copilot.

Leaders should think about use cases that tend to sit at the intersection of high repetition, clear boundaries, and measurable impact. For example, the Human Resources (HR) department needs to automate the onboarding guidance or internal request workflows. You can create a Copilot Studio agent that can reduce burden across the organization by becoming a trusted first stop, answering questions accurately, and escalating or automating only when needed. Scenarios like this work well because they're contained, auditable, and easy to improve over time. Trying to solve ambiguous, judgment-heavy work with custom agents too early can lead to over-engineering and a level of complexity that your organization may not be mature enough at this point in the AI journey to deal with.

Copilot Studio should also be viewed as a governed extension layer, not an innovation free platform. Microsoft designed it to operate with enterprise controls, analytics, and governance so organizations can scale safely. That means success isn't measured by how many agents you build; instead, success should be measured by evaluating:

- How intentionally do you deploy them
- How well they're grounded in real business needs
- How clearly they improve outcomes

In practice, the strongest Copilot Studio deployments look boring on the surface, simple agents solving real problems consistently, but transformational underneath because they quietly change how work flows across your organization. Understanding the business value of Copilot Studio is critical because it aligns directly with the "extend versus build versus buy" decision model. Use Table 2-2 to understand some important questions that should be asked when thinking about building agents:

TABLE 2-2 Decision matrix

Question to Ask the Team	Considerations	Observations
Are you solving a knowledge or workflow gap?	Consider building an agent when the problem is not informational or conversational, but transactional, event-driven, or deeply system-integrated in ways that exceed what Copilot Studio connectors and flows can handle.	If the problem is that people can't find the right information, don't understand policies, or keep asking the same questions, you should not be thinking about building custom AI.
How often does this scenario happen and for how many people?	High-frequency, repeatable scenarios are ideal for extending Copilot with Copilot Studio agents.	If the use case doesn't justify a dedicated product, it probably shouldn't be built.
Does the AI need to take actions, and how complex are those actions?	You should move toward building only when actions require custom orchestration logic, advanced AI planning, multiple autonomous agents, or non-Microsoft AI stacks.	This is beyond just task automation.
Who owns this, and can it be governed safely?	When you build custom AI solutions, ownership shifts squarely to engineering and platform teams.	Leaders should treat "build" decisions the same way they treat building a new internal system: product roadmap, support model, lifecycle plan, and risk acceptance.

Understand the capabilities of Microsoft Graph

You may think about Microsoft Graph[5] as just a set of APIs, which technically is accurate. However, from an AI and business transformation point of view, Microsoft Graph is really the connective tissue of Microsoft 365. Think about Microsoft Graph as the layer that understands all about you, such as

- Who you are
- What you work on
- Who you collaborate with

Not only that, but it also understands where information lives across emails, files, chats, meetings, devices, and security signals, as shown in Figure 2-5. All these insights are exposed through a single, consistent endpoint and permission model.

If you think about AI at scale, this approach is very important. Microsoft 365 Copilot doesn't magically "know" your organization; it relies on Microsoft Graph to ground every response in real, permission-aware data. When you ask Copilot a question like "What's the latest document for this project?"

[5] For more information about Microsoft Graph, visit *https://learn.microsoft.com/en-us/graph/overview.*

or "Summarize my open action items," what happens behind the scenes is a query to Microsoft Graph for relevant emails, SharePoint files, Teams chats, meetings, and relationships. Microsoft Graph ensures Copilot only surfaces content the user is allowed to see, honoring security boundaries.

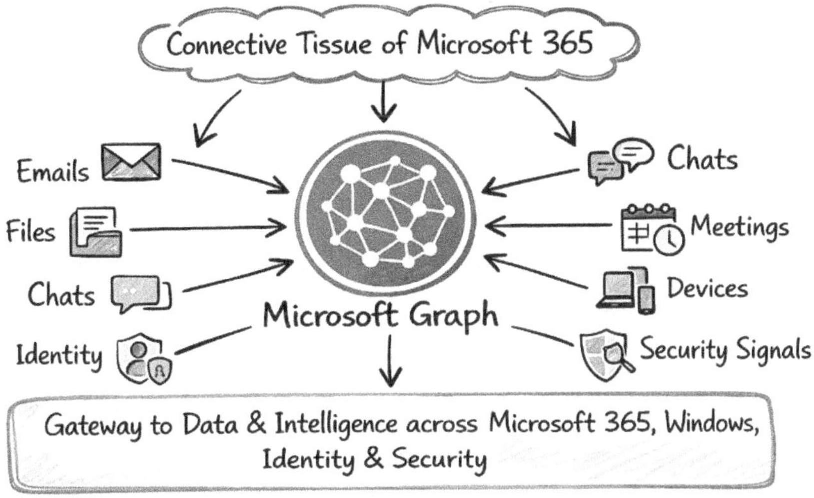

FIGURE 2-5 Microsoft Graph

As an AI transformational leader, this means establishing a clear message stating that *to improve AI outcomes, it is necessary to improve Microsoft Graph data quality*. What does this mean? An example of data quality in this context means having clean SharePoint structures, meaningful document titles, consistent permissions, and active collaboration. All these will make Microsoft Graph smarter, and when Microsoft Graph is smarter, Copilot is more useful. This is why Microsoft positions Graph not just as a developer tool, but as the foundation for productivity insights, workplace analytics, and AI-powered experiences across Microsoft 365.

This is also an important time to reflect on how to bring external data to Microsoft Graph. One option is to use the Microsoft Graph API for real-time access to data, Graph (Copilot) connectors that bring external data sources like ServiceNow, Jira, or Salesforce into Microsoft 365. Another option is the Graph Data Connect for large-scale analytics scenarios. Together, these capabilities allow organizations to extend Microsoft 365, enrich Copilot responses, and build custom AI-infused solutions while staying inside Microsoft's identity, security, and compliance boundaries.

Identify the benefits and capabilities of an integrated Microsoft AI solution, including risk mitigation and safety benefits

When talking about an integrated Microsoft AI solution, you should really be talking about something much bigger than tooling. It is actually about the ecosystem that was designed to carry your organization's identity, data, and security posture into the AI era without breaking what already works. AI introduces speed, scale, and autonomy, but it also amplifies risk if not grounded properly.

As a leader, you should see the integrated approach as an advantage, as it prevents starting from scratch. Your existing investments in identity, compliance, and security don't get bypassed; they become the control plane that governs AI behavior. As a leader, this should immediately shift your thinking from *"How do we deploy AI?"* to *"How do we extend our existing trust model into AI-driven workflows?"*

The first strategic consideration is *data exposure*. This means not just where your data lives, but also how AI interacts with it. In a Microsoft-centric architecture, services like Microsoft Graph, Microsoft Purview, and Microsoft Entra work together to ensure that AI responses are scoped to what a user is already authorized to see. This is a critical point that many times, siloed solutions cannot offer without a series of configurations and manual integration. Without that enforcement layer, Gen AI can inadvertently surface sensitive information across boundaries. From a technical standpoint, this is enforced through access control lists, sensitivity labels, and data classification policies that Copilot respects at runtime.

> **Important** From a leadership standpoint, the takeaway is simple: your AI is only as safe as your data governance maturity. If your data is overexposed today, AI will make that problem visible faster.

Next, you should also think about prompt and response safety. AI systems don't just consume data; they generate it. This introduces a new class of risks, such as hallucinations, policy violations, and prompt injection attacks. Microsoft AI solution addresses this through layered safety mechanisms, including content filtering, grounding techniques (such as retrieval-augmented generation), and continuous monitoring, as shown in Figure 2-6.

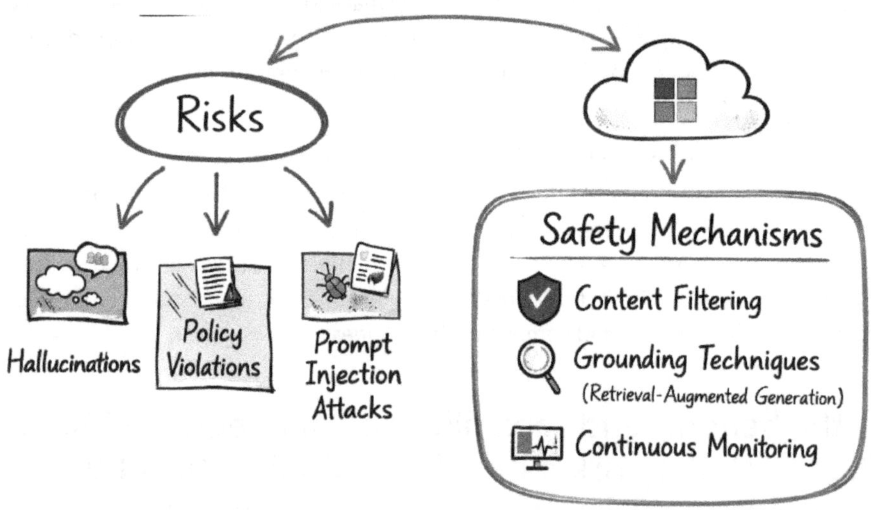

FIGURE 2-6 Safety mechanisms

Having said that, it is important to emphasize that these controls are not a replacement for governance; they are an extension of it. As a leader, you should ensure that your organization has correctly defined what "acceptable use" looks like, what outputs are allowed, and how AI-generated content is validated before it becomes business-critical. In practice, this means combining technical safeguards with policy frameworks and user education.

Another important consideration is operational visibility. This is also important because AI without observability is a blind spot waiting to happen. Microsoft AI solution provides telemetry across the AI lifecycle, which provides insights such as:

- Who is using AI
- What prompts are being submitted
- What data is being accessed
- What outputs are being generated

This visibility is essential for both security teams and business leaders. It enables anomaly detection, supports compliance audits, and helps organizations refine how AI is being used over time. From a leadership perspective, it's about ensuring that AI adoption remains measurable, accountable, and continuously improved.

There is also a broader leadership lens that often gets overlooked: *trust is the currency of AI adoption*. Employees need to trust that the system is accurate and safe. Otherwise, they will not use it. Customers also need to trust that their data is protected. Last but not least, regulators need to trust that your organization is operating responsibly. An integrated Microsoft AI solution gives you a strong foundation to build that trust, but it is not a silver bullet for trust. Trust is earned through consistent behavior, through transparency, governance, and thoughtful implementation. As a leader, you should ask yourself: Are we deploying AI in a way that strengthens trust, or are we moving too fast and risking it? That is a tactical question that will shape the future of your AI strategy.

Map business processes and use cases to Microsoft's AI apps and services

One common mistake that many leaders make when they start an AI project is by first looking at the AI Solution feature set and then trying to adapt those features to their organization's needs. Mapping business processes to an AI solution starts with understanding where work actually happens in your organization. As a leader, your role is not to start with technology, but with the friction points in the business. Where are decisions delayed? Where is knowledge fragmented? Where are people spending time on repetitive work that doesn't create value?

The idea is to reinforce a core principle that was shared in this book before, which is: *the fastest AI value comes from augmenting existing workflows (emails, meetings, document creation, analysis) rather than building net-new systems*. Leaders should look at high-frequency, knowledge-heavy processes, status reporting, proposal drafting, meeting follow-ups, and data summarization and map them to Microsoft 365 Copilot capabilities that reduce manual effort while staying within enterprise security and permission boundaries.

A practical way to approach this is to break down business processes into functional domains such as sales, operations, finance, HR, and security, and then identify how AI can augment each one. For example, in operations, Azure AI services can automate document processing and enable predictive maintenance scenarios. The key insight here is that AI should be embedded into the flow of work, not introduced as a separate system that users need to adopt.

Another important consideration is aligning the type of AI capability to the nature of the task. Not all use cases require generative AI. Some are better served by traditional machine learning or cognitive services. For example, Azure Vision in Foundry Tools is ideal for image and video analysis, while Azure AI Search enables knowledge retrieval scenarios with semantic understanding. As a leader, you need to guide your organization toward the right mix of capabilities. Let's use Table 2-3 as an example of how business processes can be mapped to Microsoft AI solutions:

TABLE 2-3 Business processes and Microsoft AI Solutions

Business Process	Department	Microsoft AI App or Service
Email summarization, follow-ups, and meeting prep	All/corporate	Microsoft 365 Copilot (Outlook, Teams)
Financial analysis, forecasting, and variance explanations	Finance	Microsoft 365 Copilot (Excel)
Budget reporting and executive presentations	Finance	Microsoft 365 Copilot (PowerPoint)
Employee onboarding and policy Q&A	Human resources	Microsoft Copilot Studio (AI agents)
Resume screening and candidate shortlisting	Human resources	Microsoft Copilot + Microsoft 365 Copilot
Customer support, self-service, and ticket triage	Customer support	Microsoft Copilot Studio + Power Automate
Workflow approvals and process automation	Operations	Power Automate with Copilot
Knowledge base search and enterprise Q&A	IT/all departments	Microsoft 365 Copilot + Microsoft Graph

As a leader, you must balance innovation with governance. Mapping use cases is not just about identifying opportunities; it's also about understanding risk, compliance, and impact. Sensitive processes, such as financial reporting or legal documentation, require stronger controls and validation mechanisms. This is where Microsoft's integrated security and compliance capabilities become essential. As you map business processes to AI, always ask: *What data is involved? Who has access? What are the risks if the AI is wrong?* These are the kinds of questions that differentiate technical implementation from a responsible AI strategy.

Identify when to use Researcher or Analyst in Copilot

By now, it should be clear to you that not all AI assistance is the same, and you will have different Microsoft AI solutions for different usage case scenarios. Researcher and Analyst reflect two very different types of thinking: exploration and interpretation. As a leader, your role is to help your organization understand when to use each, because choosing the wrong mode doesn't just slow people down; it can lead to incomplete or misleading outcomes.

Let's start with Researcher, which you should think of as your exploratory engine. You use it when the problem is not fully defined, when you need to gather information, compare perspectives, or build an understanding of a topic. Researcher is useful for tasks like:

- Market research
- Competitive analysis
- Policy reviews
- Early-stage strategy development

If you've ever sat down with a blank page trying to make sense of a complex topic, that's where Researcher excels. It enables you to go wide by pulling together insights, summarizing large volumes of information, and identifying patterns across sources. If you think about it, it is almost like you have a skilled analyst doing desk research, but at a much faster pace.

But if you need depth and precision, then you should use Analyst. Think of using Analyst when you already have data and need to extract meaning from it. Analyst is best suited for:

- Structured or semi-structured data scenarios
- Financial analysis
- Operational metrics
- Performance tracking
- Trend identification

When you use Analyst, you already have the data; you need help interpreting it. For example, if you have a dataset and want to understand anomalies, forecast trends, or generate insights, Analyst is the better choice. It operates with a more analytical mindset, focusing on accuracy, calculations, and data-driven reasoning rather than broad exploration. So, if you have folks on your team staring at rows and columns and asking, *"What is actually happening here?"*, then they should be using Analyst to help interpret that data.

> **Important** Researcher helps you form better strategic narratives by synthesizing knowledge across your organization, while Analyst helps you make defensible decisions by grounding them in data.

As a leader, you need to be aware of the best use cases for each one of these solutions. But it is also important to mention that many real-world scenarios require a combination of both modes. You might start with Researcher to understand the landscape (analyzing industry trends, for example) and then move to Analyst to evaluate your organization's internal data against those trends. The mistake I often see is teams trying to use one mode for everything. That's not how these tools were designed. As a leader, you should guide your teams to think in phases: explore first, then analyze. This structured approach not only improves outcomes but also builds confidence. Figure 2-7 has a summary of the main use case scenarios for each solution.

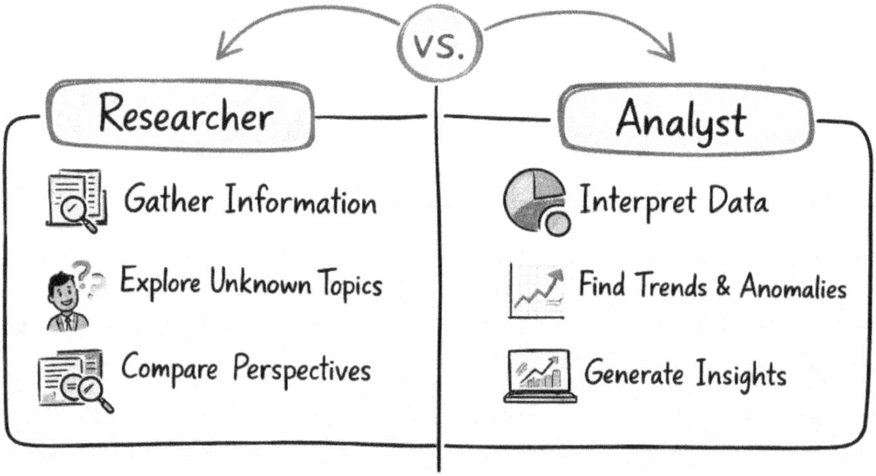

FIGURE 2-7 Key scenarios for Researcher versus Analyst

Identify when to build, buy, or extend, including the Microsoft 365 Copilot extensibility framework

As a leader, one of the most important decisions you'll make is not what AI to use, but how to adopt it. You will be challenged and ask yourself: Should we build something from scratch, buy an existing solution, or extend what we already have? This is where many organizations either accelerate their transformation or slow themselves down unnecessarily. If there's one piece of advice I'd give you early on, it's this: don't default to building. Microsoft 365 Copilot already provides a rich set of capabilities that can deliver immediate value. Your job is to understand when those capabilities are sufficient and when your business truly requires a more tailored solution.

> **Important** When leaders talk about build, buy, or extend, what they're really wrestling with is how much differentiation they need versus how quickly they need results.

Some leaders may be enticed to *buy* because it is often the fastest path to value and, in most cases, your best starting point. Microsoft 365 Copilot, along with its integrations across Word, Excel, PowerPoint, Outlook, and Teams, covers a wide range of common business scenarios. However, there will be situations where out-of-the-box functionality gets you 70–80 percent of the way there, but not quite all the way. That's where *extend* comes in, and this is where things start to get more interesting. The Microsoft 365 Copilot extensibility framework allows you to connect Copilot to your organization's data and workflows through plugins, connectors, and custom copilots built with tools like Microsoft Copilot Studio.

The next option is *build*, which should be approached with intention and discipline. That's because building your own AI solution, often using Microsoft Foundry or custom models, makes sense when you have highly specialized requirements that cannot be met through existing tools or extensions. Use Table 2-4 to compare the use case scenarios and when to choose each option:

TABLE 2-4 Build, buy, or extend

Decision	Use Case Scenario	Rationale
Build	An organization needs a highly specialized AI assistant that follows custom business rules, integrates with legacy systems, and uses a domain-specific AI model	This scenario requires full control over orchestration, data flow, and possibly the AI model itself. Building a custom agent using Copilot Studio or Microsoft Foundry services is more appropriate.
Buy	A team wants to summarize meetings, draft documents, and ask questions over emails and files already stored in Microsoft 365	This scenario is fully covered by out-of-the-box Microsoft 365 Copilot capabilities, which are designed for common productivity needs using Microsoft Graph data. Buying avoids unnecessary customization, reduces cost and governance complexity, and delivers the fastest time to value.
Extend	A company wants Copilot to answer questions using data from an external CRM system and create tickets in a service management tool from chat.	The core Copilot experience is sufficient, but it needs access to external data and actions. Extending Copilot using Graph connectors enables this without building a new AI solution.

As a leader, you need to think in terms of progression, not a one-time decision. Start with buy to establish quick wins and drive adoption. Move to extend as you identify gaps and opportunities for customization. Only build when there is a clear, justified need that aligns with business value. This layered approach not only reduces risk but also ensures that your AI strategy remains scalable and sustainable.

> **Important** AI transformation is not about how much you build; it's about how effectively you deliver value while maintaining control, security, and alignment with your organization's goals.

Identify the benefits and capabilities of Microsoft Foundry services

When you move from productivity AI (like Copilot) into Microsoft Foundry services, you're stepping into the builder layer of AI transformation. This is the stage where your organization stops just consuming AI and starts engineering intelligence directly into its applications, workflows, and customer experiences. As a leader, you should see Microsoft Foundry not as a collection of tools, but as a platform that allows you to operationalize AI at scale. While Copilot enhances user productivity, Microsoft Foundry enables organizations to create entirely new capabilities. Understanding when to move from consumption (Copilot) to creation (Microsoft Foundry) is a key leadership skill.

One of the biggest benefits of Microsoft Foundry services is flexibility. You're not locked into a single model, a single pattern, or even a single approach. You can combine prebuilt AI services, custom models, and generative AI depending on your organizational needs. This is critical because not every business problem requires the same type of intelligence. Some require perception (vision), others require retrieval (search), and others require reasoning (LLMs).

Map business processes and use cases to Microsoft Foundry services

The main shift in mindset now is not to think about tools and start thinking in terms of outcomes. As a leader, your goal is to identify where intelligence can reduce friction, improve accuracy, or accelerate decision-making. Your mental flow should always be the one shown in Figure 2-8.

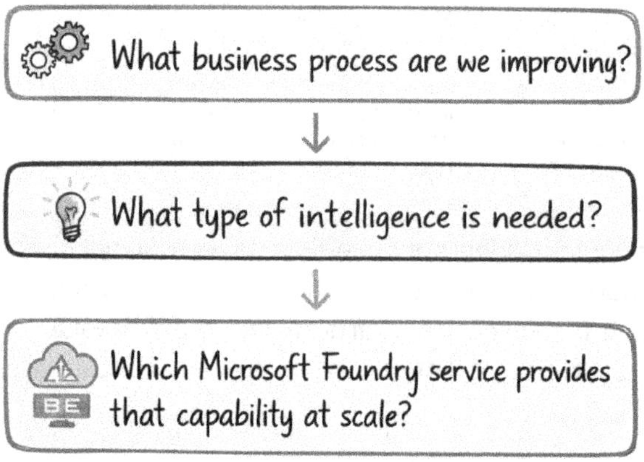

FIGURE 2-8 Mental flow for decision-making

Let's say you identified a business process that revolves around understanding or extracting meaning from unstructured content. This is the typical business process that Microsoft Foundry shines through services like Document Intelligence, Language, and Vision. For example, onboarding workflows that involve processing invoices, claims, or contracts map cleanly to Document Intelligence for structured data extraction, while customer feedback analysis maps to Language services for sentiment, classification, or summarization.

You may also identify that there are many business processes that require searching, discovering, or grounding insights across large volumes of enterprise data. This is the scenario in which Azure AI Search becomes the most appropriate solution. This is especially relevant for knowledge management, internal portals, compliance investigations, or customer support scenarios where accurate retrieval matters. Azure AI Search is often paired with generative AI to enable retrieval-augmented generation (RAG). The key leadership insight is *knowing when search precision is the real value driver.*

> **Important** As a leader, your responsibility is to recognize when off-the-shelf intelligence is no longer sufficient and a tailored solution is required.

For business processes centered on prediction, forecasting, or anomaly detection, the conversation shifts toward custom models and operational insight, where Microsoft Foundry and Azure Machine Learning come into play. Here are some typical scenarios that rely on proprietary data and require lifecycle management, governance, and monitoring:

- Demand forecasting
- Fraud detection
- Churn risk
- Predictive maintenance

Keep in mind that mapping business processes to Microsoft Foundry services is also a governance decision, not just a technical one. Microsoft Foundry services come with built-in enterprise security, compliance, and responsible AI guardrails. Microsoft consistently positions these security pillars as foundational for production-scale AI adoption. Table 2-5 has some examples of business processes and how they map to Microsoft Foundry Services.[6]

TABLE 2-5 Business processes and Microsoft Foundry services

Business Process	Recommended Azure AI Service
Document intake and processing (invoices, forms, contracts, receipts)	Azure AI Document Intelligence
Enterprise knowledge retrieval / RAG over internal content	Azure AI Search
Customer support quality improvement from call recordings	Azure AI Speech in Microsoft Foundry + Azure OpenAI Service for summarization (optional)
Image-based inspection and understanding (quality checks)	Azure Language in Foundry Tools
Identity verification / face-based workflows	Azure Vision in Foundry Tools (Face capabilities)
Multilingual communications and localization	Azure Translator in Foundry Tools
Content moderation and safety controls	Content Safety in Foundry Control Plane
Text analytics over enterprise content	Azure Language in Foundry Tools
Build a Gen AI app/agent	Azure OpenAI in Foundry Models
Enterprise-scale AI solutions that move from pilot to production	Microsoft Foundry[7]

Identify capabilities of Microsoft Foundry services, including Azure Vision in Foundry services, Azure AI Search, and Microsoft Foundry

What type of intelligence does your business need? When thinking about the capabilities offered by the different Microsoft Foundry services, your role as a leader is to bridge capabilities with real-world outcomes. Microsoft has intentionally structured services like Azure Vision in Foundry Tools, Azure

[6] For the complete list of Microsoft Foundry and the use case scenarios, visit *https://learn.microsoft.com/azure/architecture/data-guide/technology-choices/ai-services*.

[7] Microsoft Foundry is designed not just to build models, but also to operationalize AI at enterprise scale. It provides a unified platform to build, orchestrate, deploy, monitor, and govern AI applications and agents across business processes.

AI Search, and Microsoft Foundry to cover distinct but complementary layers of AI value. The key is recognizing when you need *perception* (understanding images and video), *retrieval* (finding the right information), or *orchestration* (building and governing AI solutions at scale). Figure 2-9 summarizes the use case scenario for these services.

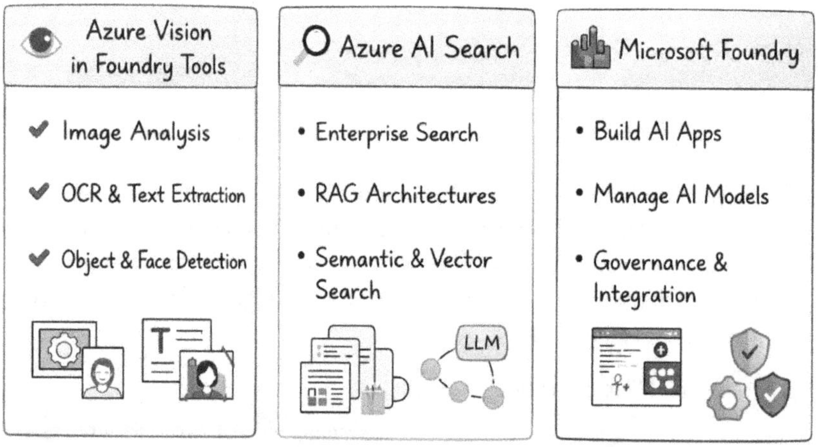

FIGURE 2-9 Use case scenario for Microsoft Foundry Services

Azure Vision in Foundry Tools brings "eyes" to your applications. This service can analyze images, extract text using Optical Character Recognition (OCR), detect objects, recognize faces (with appropriate compliance considerations), and even interpret spatial relationships in visual data. Having said that, this is not just an image processing service; the main value here is to unlock previously untapped data. Some common use case scenarios where Azure Vision in Foundry Tools transforms analog inputs into actionable insights:

- Manufacturing defects identified through image analysis
- Retail shelf monitoring
- Document digitization
- Security surveillance enhancements

Moving on to Azure AI Search, which allows you to index, enrich, and retrieve enterprise data across structured and unstructured sources. Not only that, but Azure AI Search is a foundational component for retrieval-augmented generation (RAG) architectures. Instead of relying on a model's pretrained knowledge, Azure AI Search ensures that responses are grounded in your organization's data (documents, knowledge bases, and internal systems). Keep in mind that Azure AI Search is not just about keyword matching; it includes semantic ranking,[8] vector search,[9] and AI enrichment pipelines.

[8] Read more about semantic ranking at *https://learn.microsoft.com/en-us/azure/search/semantic-search-overview.*

[9] Read more about vector search at *https://learn.microsoft.com/en-us/azure/search/vector-search-ranking.*

Now let's put everything together, and that's where Microsoft Foundry plays its role. This is a platform that enables you to design, build, test, and govern AI applications at scale. Microsoft Foundry provides access to models, tools for prompt engineering, evaluation frameworks, and integration capabilities that allow you to operationalize AI safely. It also helps you to enforce responsible AI practices, manage model lifecycles, and integrate with enterprise systems. From a leadership perspective, this is your control plane!

Match an AI model to a business need

For leaders, it is imperative to avoid the hype of choosing the mainstream model as the starting point of their organization's AI journey. Having broad knowledge of what is available in the market is important, but the real question to answer is: *What problem are we trying to solve, and what kind of intelligence does that problem require?* Remember that your job is not to pick the most advanced model; it's to pick the most appropriate one for your organization. A customer support scenario may benefit from a conversational large language model, while a fraud detection use case might require a predictive machine learning model trained on historical patterns. That's why the answer to a broader question, such as *what's the best model?* Will always be, *it depends.*

Some key concepts that were shared in Chapter 1 must come to fruition now, such as the fact that *models are only as good as the data they rely on.* This means that if your organization has rich, well-structured historical data, you can take advantage of supervised learning approaches. But if your organization's data is mostly unstructured, such as documents, emails, and images, then models that can process and reason over that type of content become more relevant.

For knowledge-heavy, language-driven tasks, such as summarization, content generation, conversational experiences, or reasoning over enterprise data, LLMs available through Azure AI platforms are more appropriate. These models are well-suited for business needs where flexibility and natural language understanding matter more than deterministic outputs. Use Table 2-6 to match the AI model with the business need.

TABLE 2-6 AI model and business need

Question the Leader Should Ask	Requirements Implied by the Question	Type of Model Recommended
Is the task primarily about understanding or generating natural language?	Needs flexibility in language, reasoning, summarization, and conversational responses; may tolerate some variability in output	Large language model (LLM)
Does this task require consistent, accurate answers grounded in enterprise data?	Requires factual accuracy, traceability, access control, and reduced hallucination risk	LLM + Retrieval-Augmented Generation (RAG) using a search or retrieval layer
Is the business input visual (images, scanned documents, video)?	Requires perception capabilities such as OCR, object detection, image, or video analysis	Task-specific vision model (computer vision/OCR models)
Does the task require reasoning across steps or coordinating actions?	Needs planning, tool use, and workflow orchestration	Agent-capable language model
Does the task depend on structured extraction rather than creative reasoning?	Needs predictable, repeatable outputs (fields, entities, layouts) with low tolerance for variation	Task-optimized model (document understanding or extraction models)

Make sure to also take into consideration operational and governance capabilities. Choosing the right model is not just a technical decision; it's a business decision that must account for security, compliance, explainability, and cost. As a leader, you should ask yourself: *Can we monitor this model effectively? Do we understand its limitations? Are we comfortable with how it handles sensitive data?* The organizations that succeed are the ones that treat model selection as part of a broader lifecycle that includes evaluation, deployment, monitoring, and continuous improvement.

Identify the benefits of Microsoft Foundry services for generative AI, including scalability and security

Now is the time to zoom out and see the bigger picture, and this bigger picture brings the realization that you're not just adopting models; you're adopting a platform that is designed to operationalize AI at enterprise scale. Microsoft Foundry gives you the building blocks to move from experimentation to production in a structured way. As a leader, your focus should be on how quickly you can go from idea to value, without compromising governance or reliability.

One of the most immediate and tangible benefits of Microsoft Foundry services is scalability. Since Gen AI workloads can be unpredictable, usage can spike based on user demand, business cycles, or even external events. Azure's cloud-native architecture allows you to scale compute, storage, and model inference dynamically, without having to provision infrastructure upfront. This elasticity is critical when deploying copilots or AI-powered applications across an entire organization. Azure also provides global availability since it operates across a vast network of regions. This allows organizations to deploy AI services closer to their users and data sources. This reduces latency and improves user experience, especially for real-time applications like chat-based assistants or AI-powered decision support systems. From a leadership perspective, this also enables you to think about AI as a global capability rather than a localized experiment. You can standardize solutions while still respecting regional requirements and performance expectations.

Security[10] is non-negotiable for enterprise generative AI. Microsoft Foundry services inherit Azure's zero-trust architecture, meaning no workload or model is trusted by default. This is particularly important for generative AI, where sensitive business data, intellectual property, and regulated information are often involved. Gen AI introduces new risks, as shown in Figure 2-10.

Azure addresses these through a layered security model that goes beyond baseline infrastructure security. Azure integrates identity, access, and governance directly into generative AI solutions. Microsoft Entra[11] plays a key role here by enabling conditional access, least privilege enforcement, and privileged identity management for AI applications and agent identities. This means leaders can control who can access AI systems, what they can do with them, and under what conditions.

---

[10] In Chapter 4, Design identity, data, and cloud security for AI solutions, you will learn more about data protection for your AI journey.

[11] More information about Microsoft Entra will be available in Chapter 4, in the section "Designing considerations for Microsoft Entra as your identity security solution for AI".

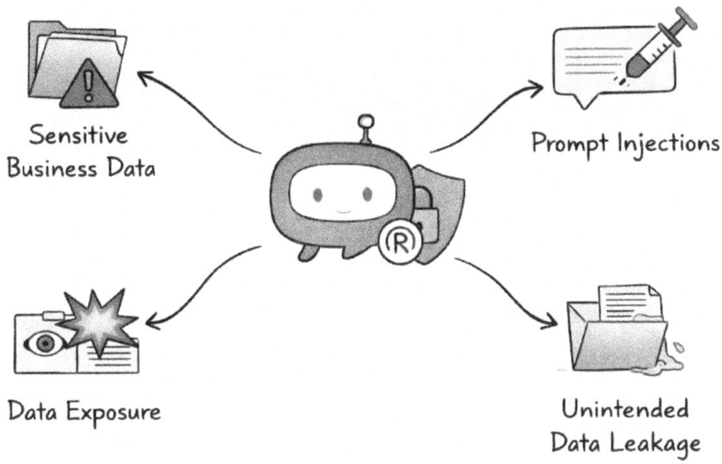

FIGURE 2-10 Some of the risks introduced with Gen AI

Beyond infrastructure and security, Microsoft Foundry services also provide strong support for responsible AI practices.[12] Tools for content filtering, monitoring, and evaluation help you manage risks associated with biased, harmful, or incorrect outputs. This is particularly important in generative AI scenarios where outputs are not deterministic. As a leader, you should think about how these capabilities fit into your broader governance framework.

> **Important** Responsible AI is not just a technical requirement; it's a leadership responsibility that shapes how your organization uses AI ethically and sustainably.

Microsoft Foundry services are designed to help organizations innovate with generative AI while maintaining trust. Customers, employees, regulators, and internal stakeholders must trust the system. Trust comes from predictable scaling, strong security, transparent governance, and alignment with responsible AI principles. Table 2-7 summarizes the Microsoft Foundry Services benefits for security and scalability:

TABLE 2-7 Microsoft Foundry Services benefits for security and scalability

Microsoft Foundry Services Capability	Benefit	Security	Scalability
Data encryption (in transit and at rest)	Protects sensitive prompts, responses, and enterprise data from unauthorized access	X	
Identity and access management (IAM) integration	Ensures only authorized users and services can access AI resources, enforcing least privilege access	X	
Private endpoints and network isolation	Enables secure communication between services without exposing traffic to the public internet	X	

12 For more information about responsible AI practices, visit *https://www.microsoft.com/en-us/ai/responsible-ai.*

Microsoft Foundry Services Capability	Benefit	Security	Scalability
Data privacy controls (no training on customer data by default)	Protects intellectual property and ensures enterprise data is not used to retrain foundation models	X	
Content filtering and safety systems	Reduces risks of harmful, biased, or policy-violating outputs in generative AI responses	X	
Responsible AI monitoring and evaluation tools	Helps detect anomalies, misuse, or unintended outputs, supporting governance and compliance	X	
Prompt shielding and protection mechanisms	Mitigates risks such as prompt injection and data exfiltration attempts	X	
Elastic compute scaling	Automatically adjusts compute resources based on demand, ensuring consistent performance during usage spikes		X
Global region availability	Allows deployment closer to users and data, reducing latency and improving responsiveness		X
Load balancing and distributed architecture	Ensures high availability and reliability for AI workloads across multiple regions		X
High-throughput model inference endpoints	Supports large volumes of concurrent requests without performance degradation		X
Model lifecycle management in Microsoft Foundry	Enables the controlled deployment, versioning, and scaling of AI models across environments		X
Integration with Azure AI Search for RAG	Scales the retrieval of enterprise data to ground AI responses across large datasets		X

From a leadership perspective, this table presents a pattern that should stand out: security features are about control and trust, while scalability features are about reach and performance. When evaluating the real value of Microsoft Foundry services, you must understand that this value comes from the combination of enabling innovation without losing governance.

Next steps

In this chapter, we explored Microsoft's AI apps and services and how to identify the benefits, capabilities, and right-fit opportunities across Copilot and Azure AI, including:

- Identifying where Microsoft 365 Copilot and Microsoft Copilot can reduce friction by embedding AI into everyday work across Word, Excel, Outlook, and Teams.
- Mapping business processes and high-frequency tasks to Copilot use cases to prioritize adoption based on impact, scale, and ease of change.
- Understanding the differences between Copilot experiences (consumer, Copilot Chat, Microsoft 365 Copilot, Copilot Studio, Security Copilot, and others) and how grounding, integration, and licensing affect outcomes.
- Explaining how Microsoft 365 Copilot Chat works across web and mobile and how it shifts from web-grounded answers to work-context grounding when licensed.

- Describing how Copilot capabilities vary by Microsoft 365 app and how those in-app experiences support drafting, analysis, summarization, and collaboration.
- Understanding when to use Copilot Studio to extend Copilot with governed, repeatable agents that connect to enterprise data and automate workflows.
- Identifying how Microsoft Graph provides permission-aware grounding and why improving Microsoft 365 data quality improves AI relevance and trust.
- Recognizing the benefits of an integrated Microsoft AI approach for risk mitigation, including data protection, governance, observability, and safety controls.
- Selecting when to use Microsoft Foundry services and how to match models to business needs, including build/buy/extend decisions and scalability and security considerations.

CHAPTER 3

Identify an implementation and adoption strategy for Microsoft's AI apps and services

"We build AI to empower people ... enable people to achieve far more."

Mustafa Suleyman, CEO of Microsoft AI

IN THIS CHAPTER, YOU WILL:

- Align an AI strategy with Microsoft's responsible AI policies
- Plan for AI adoption across the organization

Align an AI strategy with Microsoft's responsible AI policies

Across industries, failures have occurred when AI was deployed without bias testing, cross-functional oversight, and clear accountability. Without proper guardrails, you will see scenarios where AI may use discriminatory practices. For example, an agency claimed the company's recruiting software automatically rejected older applicants, specifically women over 55 and men over 60, which violates the Age Discrimination in Employment Act. This case is known to be the *Equal Employment Opportunity Commission (EEOC) v. iTutorGroup (2023),*[1] which marked the first-ever EEOC settlement involving alleged AI-driven hiring discrimination. This is where responsible AI can help to prevent these scenarios.

That's why it is important to emphasize that when you step into the role of shaping an AI strategy, success is not just measured by innovation, but also by responsible innovation. To be responsible in this space, you need to lead by example and ensure that you gain trust. Gaining trust in the technology itself is important, but trust from employees, customers, regulators, and partners who rely on the outcomes AI produces is also mandatory. This leads us to the conclusion that an AI strategy must start with trust.

Microsoft's Responsible AI framework provides a practical and principled foundation for that trust. It helps leaders move beyond experimentation into sustainable, enterprise-grade AI adoption. Microsoft

[1] Read more about this case at *https://www.akingump.com/en/insights/blogs/ag-data-dive/eeoc-settles-over-recruiting-software-in-possible-first-ever-ai-related-case?utm_source=chatgpt.com.*

Responsible AI should not be treated as a compliance afterthought; it must be used as a design principle embedded from the very beginning. As an AI transformation leader, you are expected to think beyond capability and ask deeper questions, such as: *Should we build this? How will it impact people? What could go wrong at scale?* For transformational leaders, responsible AI is what allows innovation to move fast without breaking confidence, compliance, or credibility.

This section represents a core mindset shift: AI strategy is inseparable from ethics, governance, and accountability. Responsible AI is not a compliance checkbox; it is a strategic enabler that ensures AI delivers long-term value aligned with Microsoft's principles and enterprise expectations.

> **Important** Think of responsible AI as the control plane for your strategy; it governs how models are built, deployed, monitored, and evolved. The organizations that get this right are the ones that scale AI confidently, sustainably, and ethically.

The importance of responsible AI

As AI systems increasingly influence real-world decisions, such as who gets access to opportunities, how risks are assessed, and how resources are allocated, it becomes imperative to adopt a framework that enables companies to responsibly adopt AI. But this framework is not only a moral imperative; it is a business necessity in the age of AI. When AI systems influence hiring decisions, financial approvals, healthcare outcomes, or cybersecurity defenses, the consequences of bias, error, or misuse can be severe. As a leader, your role is to ensure that AI systems are not only effective but also fair, safe, and aligned with human values. This is what separates experimental AI from enterprise-grade AI.

You should also think of Responsible AI[2] as a strategic pillar, since it directly impacts adoption. Customers and stakeholders are far more likely to embrace AI solutions when they understand how decisions are made and trust that safeguards are in place. Lack of transparency or perceived unfairness can lead to resistance, reputational damage, and even regulatory scrutiny. In other words, without responsible AI, your innovation may never reach its full potential.

As governments and international bodies are rapidly introducing AI regulations, focusing on data protection, algorithmic accountability, and risk classification, you can also think of Responsible AI as a facilitator for regulatory compliance. By embedding responsible AI principles early, you are effectively getting your organization more prepared to deal with compliance challenges and be ready to operate in a regulated AI ecosystem.

AI also introduces new categories of risk that will be covered in more detail in Chapter 4, "Design identity, data, and cloud security for AI solutions." Responsible AI can help your organization to identify, assess, and mitigate these risks systematically. For example, implementing validation pipelines and monitoring mechanisms ensures that models behave as expected even as conditions change. The principles of Microsoft Responsible AI are shown in Figure 3-1.

[2] Download the Microsoft Responsible AI Standard eBook at *https://go.microsoft.com/fwlink/?linkid=2311742*.

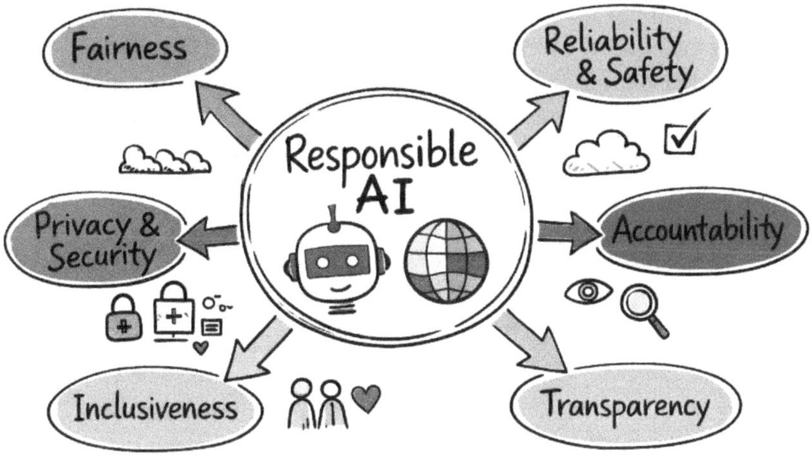

FIGURE 3-1 Principles of Microsoft Responsible AI

Table 3-1 shows more details about the principles of Microsoft Responsible AI, including the applicability in real-world scenarios:

TABLE 3-1 Responsible AI

Principle	Definition	Use case Example
Fairness	Fairness ensures that AI systems treat all people equitably and do not produce biased or discriminatory outcomes. This requires careful attention to training data, model design, and evaluation processes. Leaders must actively identify and mitigate bias, ensuring that AI systems do not reinforce existing inequalities or create new ones.	A financial services company uses AI to recommend loan approvals and routinely audits model outcomes to ensure approval rates do not unfairly disadvantage applicants based on gender or ethnicity when financial profiles are similar.
Reliability and safety	AI systems must protect personal and sensitive data through secure design, access controls, encryption, and compliance with privacy regulations.	An HR analytics platform uses encryp tion for employee data, limits access to authorized roles, and anonymizes datasets before training AI models that analyze workforce trends.
Accountability	Accountability means that humans remain responsible for AI systems and their outcomes. Organizations must define clear ownership, governance structures, and audit mechanisms to ensure that AI systems are used responsibly.	An organization assigns an AI governance board and names business owners to approve high-risk AI use cases and review incidents where AI behavior negatively impacts users.
Transparency	AI systems are understandable, and their decisions can be explained. Users and stakeholders should have visibility into how AI systems work, what data they use, and how decisions are made.	A customer service chatbot clearly informs users that responses are AI-generated and provides explanations or escalation paths.
Inclusiveness	Design AI systems that empower and serve a diverse range of users, including people with different abilities, backgrounds, and perspectives. This requires intentional design, accessibility, and considerations.	A productivity AI tool is designed with screen-reader support, voice interaction, and localization so it can be used effectively by employees with disabilities and in different global regions.
Privacy and security	AI systems must protect personal and sensitive data through secure design, access controls, encryption, and compliance with privacy regulations.	An HR analytics platform uses encryption for employee data, limits access to authorized roles, and anonymizes datasets before training AI models.

Responsible AI reinforces your organization's values and culture. It sends a clear message that innovation does not come at the expense of ethics. Keep in mind that Responsible AI is not a feature; it is a foundational principle that influences every stage of the AI lifecycle, from data collection to model deployment and beyond. With that in mind, we can represent the Responsible AI pyramid with the principles on top, followed by goals, requirements, and tools/practices as shown in Figure 3-2.

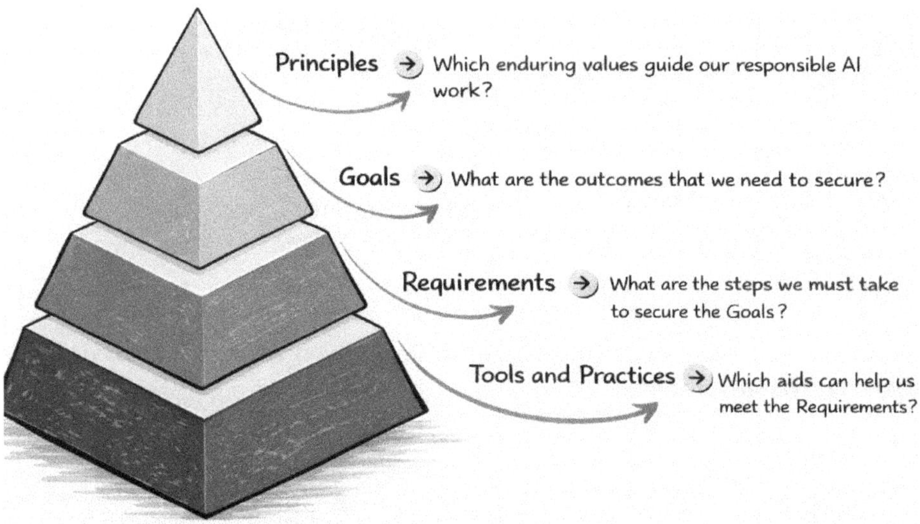

FIGURE 3-2 Responsible AI pyramid

Figure 3-2 presents a structured, layered approach to Responsible AI[3] implementation. Each level of the pyramid builds upon the one above it to ensure alignment from strategy to execution. At the top are the *Principles*, which define the enduring values that guide responsible AI work, establishing the ethical and organizational foundation. These principles inform the *Goals*, which clarify the specific outcomes the organization seeks to achieve with AI. Moving down, you have *Requirements*, which translate those goals into actionable steps, outlining what must be done to ensure the desired outcomes are realized. Finally, at the base, you have *Tools and Practices*, which provide the practical means to execute these requirements, identifying the technologies, processes, and methodologies that support implementation.

> **Important** You can apply Responsible AI regardless of your industry. But each industry will have different requirements and constraints. To learn how Responsible AI can be applied in the education industry, visit *https://learn.microsoft.com/en-us/training/paths/responsible-use-of-artificial-intelligence-in-education/*.

[3] Microsoft also offers the Responsible AI Toolbox, which has a collection of tools to help in implementing this framework. Visit *https://responsibleaitoolbox.ai/ for more information.*

Establish governance principles for AI use

Now that you understand the principles of Responsible AI, you can move forward to start planning the AI governance. As a leader, your role is to define how AI should be used, not just where it might be useful. Governance principles act as a compass, helping teams navigate trade-offs between speed, risk, and responsibility.

The first step is to define clear principles that align with both business objectives and ethical standards. These principles should address areas such as data usage, model validation, risk tolerance, and transparency requirements. They act as a guiding framework that ensures consistency across teams, especially in large enterprises where multiple AI projects may be running simultaneously. Instead of building this governance from scratch, you should use best practices from industry frameworks, such as the *Artificial Intelligence Risk Management Framework (AI RMF 1.0)*[4] from the National Institute of Standards and Technology (NIST), document *NIST AI 100-1*. Another help aid companion that you can use is the NIST AI RMF Playbook,[5] which also contains AI governance best practices.

As a leader, you need to foster a fundamental balance in which AI governance must be achieved across key organizational personas. For example, in Figure 3-3, the personas are employees, security leaders, and executive leadership. On one side, AI citizen developers are driven by speed, productivity, and the desire to quickly build solutions that automate repetitive tasks. On the other side, the CISO focuses on risk, data protection, and regulatory compliance, ensuring that innovation does not introduce vulnerabilities or expose sensitive information. At the executive level, the CIO is concerned with governance at scale, ensuring visibility, adherence to guidelines, expert validation, and measurable business value. Effective AI governance sits at the center of these competing priorities, creating a structured framework that enables innovation while enforcing guardrails.

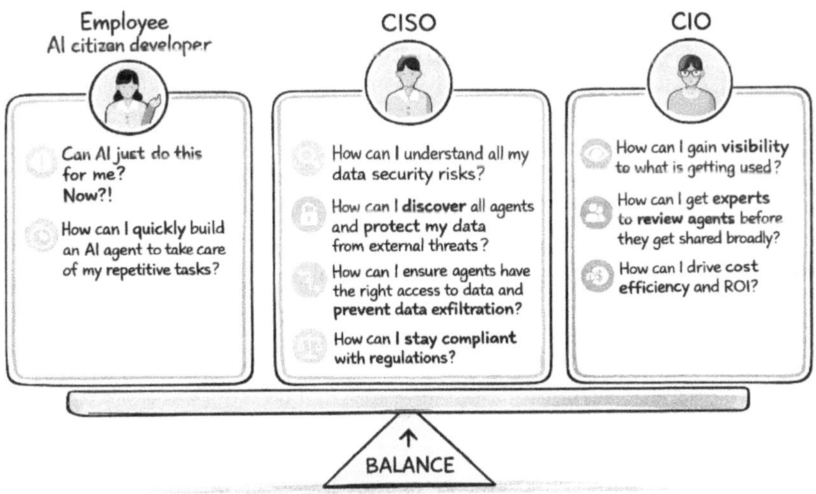

FIGURE 3-3 Creating the fundamental balance

4 Download this framework from *https://nvlpubs.nist.gov/nistpubs/ai/NIST.AI.100-1.pdf*.

5 Access the NIST AI RMF Playbook at *https://airc.nist.gov/airmf-resources/playbook/*.

The balance represented in Figure 3-3 is not static; it requires continuous alignment between agility and control, empowering organizations to scale AI responsibly without compromising security, compliance, or strategic outcomes. This balance can be challenging to achieve at first because AI systems are not static; they evolve over time. Your governance model must include processes for continuous monitoring, retraining, auditing, and decommissioning. This ensures that models remain accurate, relevant, and compliant as data and business conditions change.

When you think about documenting AI governance policies, don't approach it as a paperwork exercise. You should think of it as creating clarity for everyone involved in building and using AI. You want to make it explicit how AI is allowed to operate in your organization: what's acceptable, what's not, and under what conditions. That includes defining how data is used, how risks are assessed, and how compliance is maintained. If this isn't written down in a structured and accessible way, teams will interpret things differently, and that's when problems start to happen.

At the same time, good documentation goes beyond static policies. You should be capturing the full context of your AI systems, for example, documenting why they exist, what data they rely on, how they're evaluated, and what safeguards are in place. This creates transparency not just for audits or regulators, but also for your own teams. It allows you to scale AI with confidence because you're not reinventing governance every time a new model is deployed.

Establish an AI council to guide strategy, oversight, and cross-functional alignment

An AI council turns principles into practice. Rather than leaving AI decisions scattered across teams, the council provides centralized guidance while still allowing innovation at the edges. For transformational leaders, this is how AI strategy stays coherent as adoption scales. Think of the AI council as the orchestrator of alignment. Different roles in your organization are naturally focused on different priorities. For example, engineering teams want to build, security teams want to protect, and executives want measurable outcomes and return on investment (ROI).

The council brings these perspectives together into a single, cohesive decision-making process. It ensures that recommendations coming from operational teams are evaluated in the context of broader strategy, and that executive decisions are informed by real data, not assumptions. This is how you avoid the common trap of AI initiatives becoming fragmented or disconnected from business value.

The AI council determines what gets escalated, what requires cross-functional approval, and what can be handled within individual teams. This creates clarity and efficiency. As an AI transformational leader, your goal is not to centralize all decisions, but to ensure that the right decisions are made at the right level, with the right context.

From a governance perspective, the council also plays a key oversight role. It is responsible for ensuring that AI initiatives adhere to responsible AI principles, regulatory requirements, and organizational policies. This includes reviewing high-risk use cases, validating compliance, and monitoring outcomes over time. The council should not only approve and guide but also evaluate outcomes and feed those insights back into the strategy, as represented in Figure 3-4.

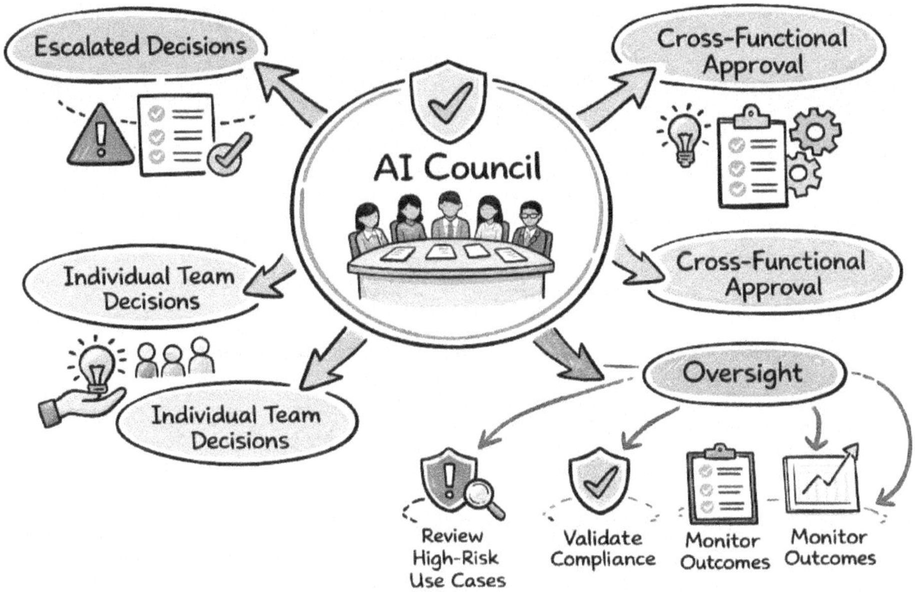

FIGURE 3-4 AI council oversight and cross-functional alignment

The council also plays a key role in education and cultural transformation. It helps raise awareness about responsible AI, provides training, and promotes a shared understanding of risks and opportunities. Table 3-2 has examples of roles, responsibilities, and outcomes that are widely reflected in AI-governance best practices from industry guidance.

TABLE 3-2 AI Council roles, responsibilities, and expected outcomes

Role	Responsibility	Expected Outcomes
Executive sponsor (such as C-suite or VP)	Sets strategic direction for AI, secures funding, and ensures AI initiatives align with business priorities and risk appetite. Acts as an escalation point for high-impact or high-risk decisions.	Clear alignment between AI investments and business strategy. Executive accountability for AI outcomes and sustained organizational commitment to responsible AI.
Business/product leader	Represents business value, customer impact, and use-case prioritization. Ensures AI initiatives solve real problems and deliver measurable outcomes.	AI use cases that are tied to business KPIs, improved adoption by business teams, and reduced risk.
AI/data science lead	Advises on model feasibility, limitations, and technical risk. Ensures AI solutions are designed with reliability, performance, and responsible AI considerations in mind.	Technically sound AI solutions, realistic expectations of AI capabilities, and early identification of model risks.
IT/architecture lead	Ensures AI solutions integrate securely and efficiently with existing platforms, data sources, and cloud services. Oversees scalability and operational readiness.	Ensures AI solutions integrate securely and efficiently with existing platforms, data sources, and cloud services. Oversees scalability and operational readiness.
Security lead (CISO or delegate)	Evaluates AI solutions for security threats, misuse, and adversarial risks. Ensures alignment with security-by-design and zero-trust principles.	Reduced AI-related security incidents, secure deployment of AI services, and improved resilience against misuse or data leakage.

Role	Responsibility	Expected Outcomes
Change management/ HR representative	Oversees workforce impact, skills readiness, and responsible AI adoption across employees. Manages communication, training, and cultural change.	Higher AI adoption rates, reduced employee resistance, and a clearer understanding of how AI supports and does not replace human work.
User or stakeholder representative	Brings the voice of end users or affected groups into AI decisions.	AI solutions that better meet user needs, have fewer unintended negative impacts, and an improved trust in AI-driven decisions.

You can use this table as a reference while putting together the team that will be part of the AI council. This council reinforces executive accountability by formally overseeing AI strategy and risk. As a leader, you want to ensure that the creation of this council will signal that responsible AI is embedded in decision-making, not delegated or ignored.

Plan for AI adoption across the organization

By now, you should already know that AI adoption across an organization is not a technology rollout; it is a transformation of how work gets done. This means that if you approach it as a simple deployment of tools, you will likely see limited impact. The goal is to approach it as a shift in mindset, processes, and decision-making, which is when AI becomes highly impactful.

Working with customers across the globe allowed me to also see that most of the AI adoption challenges that can lead to failure or delay in seeing results, will happen not because of models, prompts, or infrastructure. Most of the time, it fails because organizations underestimate the human, operational, and governance dimensions of change. Planning for AI adoption is about intentionally guiding people, processes, and platforms through a transformation that affects how work gets done at every level.

As a leader, your role is to align stakeholders, prepare your workforce, address concerns early, and ensure that governance is embedded from the beginning. AI adoption is not owned by IT alone; it is a cross-functional effort. It touches business units, security teams, compliance, and executive leadership. The organizations that succeed are the ones that treat AI adoption as a shared responsibility.

Establish an adoption team

In the previous section, you learned more about key aspects of assembling an AI council with different stakeholders from your organization. While this was a good exercise, now you are in a different stage, and you need to establish the adoption team, which is the team that acts as the central engine that drives AI initiatives forward. This team ensures alignment between business goals and technical execution. Without a dedicated team, AI efforts tend to become fragmented, with different departments experimenting in isolation and failing to scale. This team is usually responsible for five domains:

- **Use-case prioritization**: Deciding where AI adds value and where it does not
- **Enablement and training**: Helping people learn by doing, not by policy
- **Risk and governance alignment:** Ensuring responsible AI is used

- **Measurement and feedback**: Tracking adoption, outcomes, and friction
- **Change orchestration**: Coordinating communication with AI Champions and iteration cycles

When it comes to enablement and training, you can use the 70-20-10 development philosophy. This means 70 percent of learning comes from hands-on experience, 20 percent from exposure to others (collaboration or coaching), and 10 percent from formal training. This model also helps to identify users who can become AI Champions, as we will discuss more in the next section.

As you think about the members of this team, you should keep in mind that it must be cross-functional by design. In other words, it needs to include representatives from IT, security, data, compliance, and key business units. Figure 3-5 represents some key areas that must be represented in the AI Adoption Team.

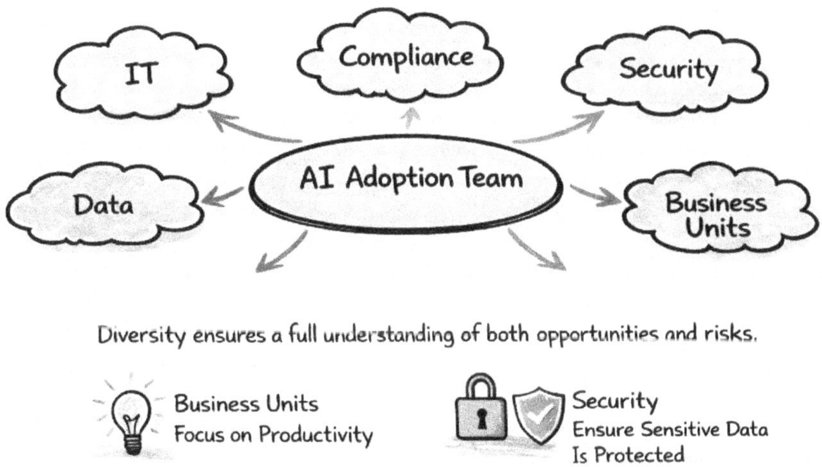

FIGURE 3-5 AI Adoption Team

While this diversity of team members is imperative, it is equally important to have a leadership sponsor. The adoption team should have a clear executive sponsor who can remove blockers, secure funding, and communicate the strategic importance of AI initiatives. Without executive backing, even the most promising AI projects can struggle to gain traction. Once you assemble this team, you need to define clear roles and responsibilities, which can be bucketized in decision areas. Table 3-3 has some examples of questions to ask per decision area.

TABLE 3-3 Decision area questions

Decision Area	Common Questions	Why It Matters?
Strategy and use-case ownership	■ Who prioritizes and deprioritizes AI use cases across the organization? ■ Who defines success criteria for each use case (KPIs, productivity gains, risk thresholds)? ■ Who decides when a use case is ready to move from pilot to scaled deployment? ■ Who has the authority to stop or retire an AI use case if value or risk changes?	Without explicit answers here, organizations accumulate AI pilots that never scale—or worse, keep running without business ownership.

Decision Area	Common Questions	Why It Matters?
Governance, risk, and responsible AI	■ Who defines what "acceptable AI use" means in this organization? ■ Who owns Responsible AI alignment? ■ Who approves high-risk use cases (e.g., HR, legal, customer-facing automation)? ■ Who owns ongoing monitoring once AI is in production? ■ Who is accountable if an AI system causes harm, bias, or regulatory exposure?	Enterprise AI governance accountability must be assigned, not assumed. Regulators and boards increasingly expect named owners, not shared responsibility.
Data, security, and privacy	■ Who decides which data sources AI systems are allowed to access? ■ Who validates data quality and suitability for AI use? ■ Who owns privacy impact assessments for AI-enabled workflows? ■ Who defines data retention, logging, and audit requirements for AI interactions? ■ Who approves AI access to sensitive or regulated data (PII, IP, financial data)?	Most AI risk does not come from the model; it comes from data misuse or over-permission.
Adoption, enablement, and culture	■ Who owns end-user adoption and behavior change? ■ Who defines training strategy (role-based vs. generic)? ■ Who establishes and runs the AI Champions program? ■ Who collects and acts on user feedback and friction signals?	Studies[6] show that employees often pretend to use AI or quietly abandon tools when guidance is unclear. Clear ownership prevents this invisible failure mode.
Financial management and cost control	■ Who owns AI spend visibility across licenses, usage, and consumption models? ■ Who defines budgets, thresholds, and guardrails for AI usage? ■ Who is accountable for ROI measurement and value realization? ■ Who decides when to scale up or scale back AI investments?	Boards and executives increasingly ask for AI ROI[7] clarity. Cost ownership ambiguity is one of the fastest ways to lose executive support for AI programs.

Important If the AI Adoption Team cannot clearly answer "who owns this?" the organization is not ready to scale AI responsibly. Make sure to always answer these questions before moving forward.

Identify common barriers to adoption

If you have been in the IT field for a long time, you probably remember how difficult it was to make users, and even decision-makers, embrace cloud computing. The fear of uncertainty and the aversion to change delayed cloud adoption in many parts of the world. Yes, because many times it was a cultural

6 For more information about one of these studies, visit *https://www.howdy.com/blog/AI-fatigue-statistics*.

7 There are many studies that cover how to calculate AI ROI. One that you can use as a reference is *https://www.bcg.com/publications/2025/how-finance-leaders-can-get-roi-from-ai*; although it is tailored for the finance sector, it can give you a perspective of what to measure.

reflection. I remember going to TechEd Madrid in 2014 to talk about cloud computing, and the level of resistance from the audience was tremendous. Nowadays, with AI, we are going through a similar cycle. Reality is that most significant barriers are rarely technical. They are human, organizational, and cultural. If you take one lesson from this section, let it be this: AI adoption fails more often because of people and processes than because of models and algorithms. A study[8] released in 2025 highlighted that up to 95 percent of generative AI initiatives fail to deliver expected outcomes, not due to model limitations, but because of gaps in organizational learning and integration. This is a very important insight for an AI transformation leader. This means your success will depend less on choosing the "best model" and more on how effectively you prepare your organization to use it.

Human resistance plays a big role in adopting AI and is usually the main barrier. Employees may not openly reject AI, but they may avoid using it, question its outputs, or quietly revert to old ways of working. A 2025 study conducted by the Pew Research Center[9] concluded that 63 percent of workers use AI minimally or not at all, despite the widespread availability of tools. People fear what they don't understand. Some worry that AI will replace them, while others fear making mistakes by relying on AI outputs. And some others, simply don't trust the accuracy of AI-generated content. As a leader, your role is not to force adoption; it is to build confidence.

> **Important** AI adoption accelerates when people feel empowered, not threatened. As a leader, make sure you provide a safe environment to experiment, encourage human-in-the-loop validation, and frame AI as augmentation, not replacement.

In 2025, a survey of more than 1,000 IT decision-makers in the UK[10] found that *lack of expertise* is one of the top barriers to AI adoption, particularly in large organizations. This includes not only technical skills, but also practical skills such as prompt engineering, critical evaluation of outputs, and understanding limitations.

Another major adoption barrier is *leadership perception versus employees' reality.* In a study (The State of Digital Adoption 2026) conducted in 2026 by WalkMe found that while 88 percent of executives believed employees had the right tools, only 21 percent of employees agreed with that. To mitigate this barrier it is imperative to invest in continuous training programs, hands-on learning experiences, and role-specific AI education. These mitigations should be driven by the AI Adoption Team with full sponsorship from the executive board.

Aside from the common barriers mentioned above, some other challenges for AI adoption include the ones shown in Table 3-4:

---

8 Read more about it here *https://fortune.com/2025/08/18/mit-report-95-percent-generative-ai-pilots-at-companies-failing-cfo.*

9 Read more at *https://www.pewresearch.org/social-trends/2025/02/25/workers-exposure-to-ai/.*

10 Read more at *https://www.techuk.org/resource/major-barriers-to-ai-adoption-remain-for-uk-businesses-despite-growing-demand-new-report-reveals.html.*

TABLE 3-4 AI adoption barriers and countermeasures

Adoption Barrier	Description	Mitigation
Data quality	You probably heard that AI is only as good as the data it relies on. In many scenarios, data quality becomes a barrier that many organizations face. Data quality comes from issues related to data fragmentation, inconsistency, lack of classification, or just poorly governed.	Ensure that data is properly classified, access is controlled, and sensitive information is protected.
Organizational silos and lack of strategy	Many organizations approach AI adoption in a fragmented way. Different teams experiment independently, creating isolated solutions that do not scale. This lack of coordination leads to duplication, inefficiencies, and inconsistent governance.	AI transformation requires alignment across business units, IT, security teams, data, and compliance functions. Ensuring that this alignment exists helps mitigate this barrier.
Cost and ROI uncertainty	Another barrier that often slows adoption is uncertainty around cost and return on investment. AI initiatives can start small, but they scale quickly, and so do their costs.	Make sure to define clear success metrics early and track both quantitative and qualitative outcomes. Lastly, treat AI as a long-term investment, not a quick win.
Adoption gap from pilot to scale	One of the biggest challenges is moving from experimentation to enterprise-wide adoption. Many organizations successfully run AI pilots, but very few scale them.	Make sure to have strong data foundations, integration with existing workflows, clear ownership, and accountability.

Establish an AI Champions program

As mentioned earlier in this chapter, part of a successful adoption plan is to ensure that the organization has an AI culture. Creating an AI culture goes beyond training sessions, emails, or executive mandates. You need people inside the organization who believe in it, experiment with it, and most importantly, help others see its value in their own day-to-day work. This is where an AI Champions program becomes one of the most powerful tools in your adoption strategy.

You should think of AI Champions as your multipliers. They are not part of the central AI team, but they extend its reach across the entire organization. AI Champions can sit inside business units, understand real workflows, and translate abstract AI capabilities into practical, meaningful use cases. Without them, adoption tends to remain centralized and slow, but with them, it becomes organic.

One important point to keep in mind is that the AI Champions program is not just about identifying enthusiastic individuals and giving them access to tools. It is about building a structured, intentional network of advocates who are empowered, supported, and aligned with your organization's broader AI strategy. While there are many ways to build an effective AI Champions program, we will focus on the following stages of the program:

- Establish the right mindset for the program
- Define the role clearly
- Provide structured enablement
- Create a feedback loop

- Offer recognition and rewards
- Align champions with real business outcomes
- Scale the program thoughtfully
- Make it part of your organization's culture

These stages can help you to successfully establish the program. An AI Champions program, when done right, can accelerate adoption, improve outcomes, and even influence culture. On the other hand, if it's done poorly, it becomes another initiative that fades away after initial excitement. Let's see more details about these stages!

Establish the right mindset for the program

One of the most common mistakes organizations make is selecting champions based purely on technical expertise. While technical knowledge can be helpful, it is not the most important trait. The best champions are those who are

- Curious and willing to experiment
- Respected by their peers
- Comfortable sharing knowledge
- Open to learning and adapting

As part of identifying who the AI Champions will be, you need to identify individuals who will act as bridges between the central AI strategy and the reality of business operations. They must understand the language of their teams, the constraints of their workflows, and the challenges their colleagues face.

> **Important** As you build your program, focus less on "who knows AI" and more on who can influence others to use AI effectively.

Define the role clearly

A rule of thumb for any adoption program is that ambiguity is the enemy of adoption. If AI Champions don't know what is expected from them, they will default to passive participation. In other words, you must clearly define the goals. What does it mean to be an AI Champion in your organization? Here are examples of tasks that can be used to set the right expectation:

- Promoting AI tools within their teams
- Sharing best practices and use cases
- Providing feedback to the central AI team
- Supporting colleagues with basic questions
- Identifying new opportunities for AI

Clarity here is essential, especially for scaling. When every champion understands their role, the program becomes consistent across departments.

Provide structured enablement

AI Champions must be prepared to advocate for AI, and this means ongoing readiness. They need early access to AI tools (such as Copilot) and a roadmap, hands-on workshops focused on real scenarios, guidance on prompt engineering, and a clear understanding of responsible AI principles. Since AI evolves fast, you could think of disseminating readiness to AI Champions via monthly enablement sessions, internal knowledge sharing forums, and weekly newsletters.

Create a feedback loop

Users need to understand that their voices are heard, and AI Champions play a big role in funneling users' feedback to the adoption team. With surveys asking what is working or not as a vehicle for feedback, AI Champions can capture many meaningful insights: for example, understand which scenarios are not being adopted, how users are struggling with AI, and identify new use cases.

Without this feedback loop, you risk operating in the dark, making decisions based on assumptions rather than real-world insights. You should approach this task with the continuous improvement mindset that strengthens your entire AI adoption strategy, as highlighted in Figure 3-6.

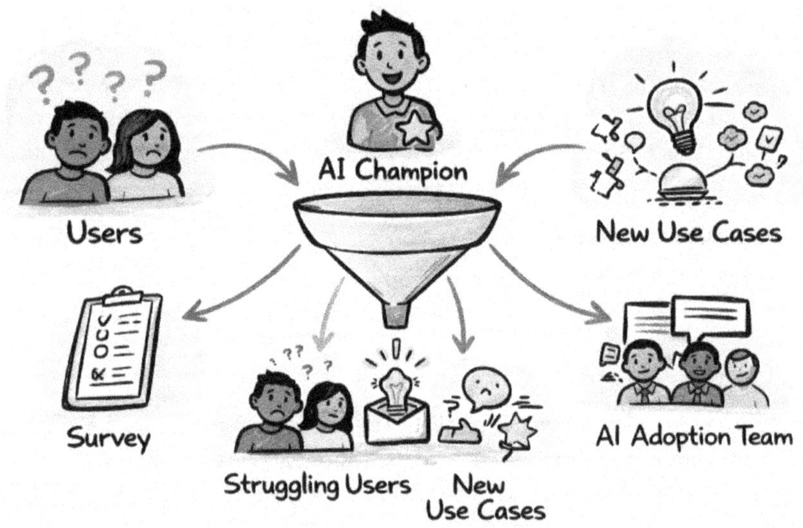

FIGURE 3-6 Inputs from the feedback loop

Offer recognition and awards

Let's be honest; AI Champions will need to take additional responsibilities on top of their existing roles, and if their contributions are not recognized, motivation will decline over time. But recognition does not always have to be financial. As a matter of fact, as a manager of a global team, I have often seen my direct reports be well-motivated when I gave them the right level of visibility and acknowledgment for the great work they did.

Often, it is about creating a structured recognition program that includes formal awards programs (like issuing a Credly badge), providing opportunities for them to present their work to leadership, and including their contributions in performance evaluations. When recognition is done well, it creates a ripple effect, which leads to more employees becoming interested in participating, and the program grows organically.

Align champions with real business outcomes

One of the biggest risks in any adoption program is focusing too much on the tool and not enough on the outcome. Unfortunately, I've seen many times companies measuring only AI usage, and that's not the right approach. AI Champions should not be measured by how often they use AI; they should be measured by the impact they help create. Encourage champions to focus on:

- Reducing time spent on repetitive tasks
- Improving quality of outputs
- Enabling faster decision-making
- Enhancing customer experiences

Scale the program thoughtfully

As your AI adoption grows, your champions program will need to scale with it. But scaling should be intentional. You should start small by identifying a core group of champions, testing your approach, and refining it. Once you have a working model, expand gradually. Some guidelines to scale include:

- Creating tiers of champions (beginner, advanced, and the like)
- Assigning champions to specific business units
- Establishing regional or functional leads

Understand Copilot license types, including pay-as-you-go, monthly, and included with a Microsoft 365 subscription

One of the items that is always top of mind for leaders is how much AI will cost for their organization. Multiple industry studies highlight a consistent concern among executives: while AI adoption is accelerating, measurable return on investment remains vague. Surveys from PwC[11] and Deloitte[12] show that more than half of CEOs are not yet seeing meaningful financial impact. At the same time, CIOs acknowledge that ROI for generative AI is difficult to quantify.

[11] Read more about the PwC Study at *https://www.pwc.com/gx/en/issues/c-suite-insights/ceo-survey.html.*

[12] Read more about the Deloitte Study at *https://www.deloitte.com/nl/en/issues/generative-ai/ai-roi-the-paradox-of-rising-investment-and-elusive-returns.html.*

While this scenario may sound alarming, the reality is often that the lack of clarity around ROI is not a limitation of AI itself; it is a failure of planning, strategy, and visibility before adoption. If you're leading AI transformation, you need to think about licensing not as a procurement exercise, but as a strategic lever for adoption. The licensing model you choose will directly influence who uses AI, how often they use it, and how quickly adoption spreads. In many ways, licensing becomes the bridge between ambition and execution.

Microsoft Copilot offerings introduce a mix of licensing approaches, including bundled capabilities within Microsoft 365, monthly per-user subscriptions, and pay-as-you-go consumption models. Each of these serves a different purpose, and understanding when to use each one is critical, not just for cost control, but also for enabling meaningful business outcomes.

Choosing your license model

Let's start with the monthly model. Monthly, per-user Copilot subscriptions represent the next level of commitment. These licenses are typically assigned to users who are expected to use AI regularly as part of their daily workflows. From a leadership perspective, this model offers two major advantages: predictability and intentional deployment. This predictability is especially important when scaling AI across departments. Intentional deployment approach helps generate early wins, which can then be used to justify broader rollout.

Pay-as-you-go models introduce a different dimension to AI consumption. Instead of paying per user, organizations pay based on usage, typically measured in tokens, API calls, or compute consumption. This license model provides flexibility, but it also introduces variability. In other words, costs can scale quickly if usage is not monitored carefully. This is why governance and cost management have become critical when using consumption-based models.

Now that you have a perspective on both, you still don't have to settle with one. As a matter of fact, one of the biggest misconceptions is that organizations must choose a single licensing model. In reality, the most effective strategies combine multiple models. As a leader, your job is to orchestrate these models together in a way that aligns with your business goals. For example:

- Start with bundled capabilities to introduce AI
- Use champions to identify high-value use cases
- Expand with subscription licenses for key roles
- Enable innovation teams with pay-as-you-go models

This layered approach ensures both scale and depth. Now take a look at some common use case scenarios for both license models in Table 3-5.

TABLE 3-5 License model scenarios

License Model	Recommended Use Case	Advantages
Pay-as-you-go (consumption-based)	Best for experimentation, pilots, and custom AI agents built with Copilot Studio. Also suitable when usage is unpredictable or when extending AI to large audiences without per-user licensing. Common in scenarios such as FAQ agents, HR or IT help desk bots, policy assistants, and workflow automation exposed to many users.	■ Low commitment, high flexibility—pay only for actual usage rather than pre-allocating licenses. ■ Scales elastically with demand, making it ideal for pilots and innovation. ■ Enables broad reach (many users can interact with an agent without each needing a Copilot license). ■ Strong fit for cost-controlled experimentation when paired with Azure budgets and alerts.
Monthly subscription (per-user license)	Best for core productivity roles that need deep integration with Microsoft 365 apps (Word, Excel, PowerPoint, Outlook, Teams). Recommended for leaders, managers, analysts, and knowledge workers where Copilot is used daily for creation, analysis, and decision support.	■ Predictable cost model, easy to budget and forecast. ■ Deep, work-grounded capabilities through Microsoft Graph (emails, files, meetings, chats). ■ Faster time to productivity gains for individual users. ■ Simplifies governance by tying usage and value to clearly defined roles.

Microsoft 365 Copilot is the paid add-on license that most leaders think of when they hear "Copilot." It is licensed per user, per month, and requires a qualifying Microsoft 365 base license such as Business Standard, Business Premium, E3, E5, or E7 (where applicable). Microsoft 365 Copilot Chat is included at no additional cost with many Microsoft 365 Business and Enterprise plans. What Copilot Chat does not do is access Microsoft Graph data (emails, documents, meetings, or Teams chats) unless a paid Microsoft 365 Copilot license is assigned.

If you step back, Copilot licensing is not just about cost; it is about enabling the right people to use the right capabilities at the right time. As a leader, you are not managing licenses; you are shaping how AI becomes part of your organization's DNA. In summary, treat licensing as a strategic decision that drives adoption, innovation, and long-term success.

Now, let's circle back on how AI Champions have a critical role in ensuring that licensing decisions translate into real adoption. AI Champions can help to

- Identify which users need advanced capabilities
- Demonstrate value to justify additional licenses
- Provide feedback on usage patterns
- Surface underutilized licenses

While it is a leadership decision to choose the license model (from the strategic standpoint), use the feedback loop to understand users' needs. AI Champions can ensure that licensing evolves based on real-world usage, not assumptions. Most successful organizations will turn licensing into a competitive advantage by using the stages described in Figure 3-7.

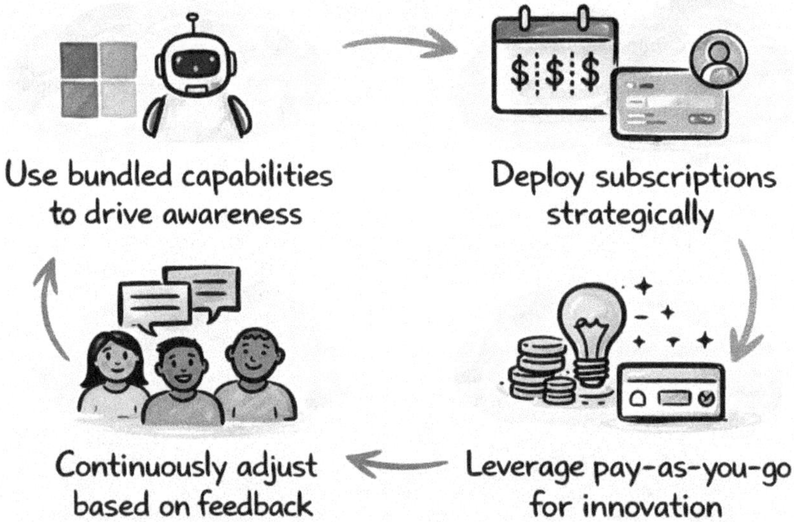

FIGURE 3-7 Adopting the right license according to AI adoption and demands

Understand Microsoft Foundry services subscription models, including pay-as-you-go and provisioned throughput unit (PTU)

Unlike storage or virtual machines, AI inference is not a steady, linear workload. A single burst of prompts can generate millions of tokens in seconds, while long periods may pass with little activity. Microsoft Foundry services, including Azure OpenAI in Foundry Models, are therefore priced around usage intensity, not just uptime.

This means that with Microsoft Foundry services, you are entering a model where usage directly translates into cost, and where cost must be carefully aligned with value. Unlike traditional enterprise software, where licensing is often fixed and predictable, Microsoft Foundry introduces a more dynamic model. You are now working with compute-driven, data-driven, and interaction-driven consumption patterns.

This creates both opportunity and risk. Opportunity, because you can scale precisely as needed. Risk, because without visibility and governance, costs can grow faster than expected. As a leader, your responsibility is to understand not just what Microsoft Foundry services can do, but also how users can consume this service, and how the consumption of these services aligns with business outcomes.

Without governance and cost visibility, AI spending becomes unpredictable and materially impacts profitability. Gartner Research[13] indicates that through 2028, at least 50 percent of generative AI projects are expected to exceed their budgeted costs due to poor architectural decisions and a lack of operational discipline. Without proper planning and governance, AI initiatives often become financially unsustainable.

---

[13] Read more about this at *https://www.truefoundry.com/blog/the-real-cost-of-generative-ai.*

Choosing the right license model for your organization

Pay-as-you-go is the default entry point for Microsoft Foundry services. In this model, you pay only for the resources your AI workload consumes, most measured in tokens (input and output) for large language models. Microsoft describes this model as Standard (On-Demand) pricing for Azure OpenAI in Foundry Models, with charges applied per token processed. There are no minimum usage commitments and no long-term contracts.

From a leadership perspective, pay-as-you-go is about optionality. It allows teams to explore, learn, and iterate without a financial lock-in. It also reduces the risk of sunk cost when a use case fails to deliver value, a common occurrence in early AI initiatives.

You can start with pay-as-you-go, and once an AI workload proves valuable and demand stabilizes, your organization may want to rethink your license strategy. In general, organizations shift toward reserved capacity. In Azure OpenAI in Foundry Models, this takes the form of provisioned throughput units (PTUs). PTUs allow organizations to reserve a fixed amount of model throughput at a fixed cost, billed hourly, monthly, or annually.

> **Important** From a leadership standpoint, prepaid models shift AI from "experiment" to operational capability. They reflect confidence that AI is now a core part of how the business runs.

While Azure OpenAI in Foundry Models is the most discussed example in this section, the same subscription principles apply across Microsoft Foundry services more broadly, such as Azure Vision in Foundry Tools, Speech, Language, and Search. Most of these services also use consumption-based pricing, often with free tiers and volume discounts. The leadership lesson remains consistent: start with flexibility; move to commitment only when value is proven. Now take a look at some common use case scenarios for both license models in Table 3-6.

TABLE 3-6 License model scenarios for Microsoft Foundry Services

License Model	Common Use Case Scenario	Advantages
Pay-as-you-go	■ AI experiments, pilots, and proofs of concept ■ Development and test environments ■ Workloads with unpredictable or bursty demand ■ Early-stage customer support bots, internal assistants, or ad-hoc analytics ■ Innovation teams exploring multiple models and use cases simultaneously	■ Maximum flexibility—no upfront commitment or long-term reservation ■ Low barrier to entry, ideal for learning and exploration ■ Cost scales directly with actual usage ■ Enables rapid iteration and fast time-to-value ■ Lower financial risk if a use case fails to deliver

License Model	Common Use Case Scenario	Advantages
PTU	■ Production workloads with stable, predictable traffic ■ Customer-facing AI requiring consistent latency and throughput ■ Mission-critical business processes powered by AI ■ Mature AI solutions with clear demand forecasts ■ Enterprise scenarios where finance requires cost certainty	■ Predictable, fixed costs that simplify budgeting and forecasting ■ Guaranteed performance (throughput and latency) ■ Often lower unit cost at scale compared to on-demand usage ■ Signals that AI is a core operational capability, not an experiment

Next steps

In this chapter, we explored how leaders can build an implementation and adoption strategy for Microsoft's AI apps and services by combining responsible AI, governance, organizational readiness, licensing strategy, and cost-aware consumption models. The key message is that successful AI transformation is not only about deploying technology; it requires trust, accountability, cross-functional alignment, clear ownership, and a practical path for scaling AI responsibly across the organization.

- **Align an AI strategy with Microsoft's responsible AI policies:** Responsible AI is positioned as the foundation for trustworthy AI adoption. The chapter explains that AI strategy must account for fairness, reliability, safety, accountability, transparency, inclusiveness, privacy, and security from the beginning, rather than treating ethics and compliance as afterthoughts.
- **The importance of responsible AI:** Responsible AI is presented as both a moral and business requirement because AI systems can influence hiring, finance, healthcare, cybersecurity, and other high-impact decisions. The section emphasizes that responsible AI improves trust, supports regulatory readiness, reduces risk, and helps organizations scale AI with confidence.
- **Establish governance principles for AI use:** Governance principles help organizations define how AI should be used, who owns decisions, how data and models are validated, and how risk is managed over time. The chapter highlights the need to balance innovation, productivity, security, compliance, and executive oversight through clear policies and continuous monitoring.
- **Establish an AI council:** An AI council provides cross-functional oversight, so AI decisions are not fragmented across teams. The council aligns business, engineering, security, compliance, data, change management, and user perspectives to review high-risk use cases, guide strategy, validate outcomes, and reinforce executive accountability.
- **Plan for AI adoption across the organization:** AI adoption is framed as an organizational transformation rather than a technology rollout. Leaders must prepare people, processes, and platforms together, ensuring that adoption is treated as a shared responsibility across business units, IT, security, compliance, and executive leadership.

- **Establish an adoption team:** The adoption team acts as the operating engine for AI initiatives by prioritizing use cases, enabling training, aligning with governance, measuring adoption, and orchestrating change. The chapter emphasizes that this team must be cross-functional, sponsored by leadership, and clear about ownership across strategy, risk, data, adoption, and cost control.
- **Identify common barriers to adoption:** The chapter explains that AI adoption often fails because of human, organizational, and cultural barriers rather than technical limitations. Common obstacles include resistance to change, lack of expertise, leadership perception gaps, poor data quality, organizational silos, cost uncertainty, and difficulty moving from pilots to scaled deployment.
- **Establish an AI Champions program:** AI Champions help turn centralized AI strategy into local adoption by supporting teams, sharing practical use cases, collecting feedback, and building confidence. The chapter recommends selecting champions for curiosity, influence, and willingness to help others; defining their role clearly; enabling them continuously; recognizing their contributions; and aligning their work with measurable business outcomes.
- **Understand Copilot license types:** Copilot licensing is positioned as a strategic adoption lever, not just a procurement decision. The chapter compares bundled Microsoft 365 capabilities, monthly per-user Copilot subscriptions, and pay-as-you-go models, explaining that organizations often need a layered approach that matches licensing to user roles, business value, adoption maturity, and usage patterns.
- **Understand Microsoft Foundry subscription models:** Microsoft Foundry and Azure OpenAI in Foundry Models require cost visibility because AI consumption can fluctuate based on tokens, traffic patterns, and workload intensity. The chapter contrasts pay-as-you-go for experimentation and unpredictable demand with provisioned throughput units for stable, production-grade workloads that require predictable cost, throughput, and latency.

CHAPTER 4

Design identity, data, and cloud security for AI solutions

"We need to treat AI systems with the same rigor we apply to critical infrastructure."

Dario Amodei, CEO of Anthropic

IN THIS CHAPTER, YOU WILL:

- Designing considerations for Microsoft Entra as your identity security solution for AI
- Designing considerations for Microsoft Purview as your data protection solution for AI
- Designing considerations for Microsoft Defender for Cloud as your cloud security solution for AI

Designing considerations for Microsoft Entra as your identity security solution for AI

The expansion of AI agents is accelerating rapidly. Gartner[1] forecasts that by the end of 2026, around 40 percent of enterprise applications will incorporate task-focused AI agents. This expansion is also driven by leaders who believe in Agentic AI as a competitive advantage. According to research from Capgemini Research Institute,[2] 93 percent of executives believe that organizations capable of effectively scaling AI agents within the next year will secure a competitive advantage over their peers. But, in the middle of all this Agentic AI explosion, come also lots of concerns related to security risks introduced by Agentic AI. A 2026 enterprise security analysis[3] highlights that AI agent sprawl creates fragmented environments with duplicate agents, inconsistent permissions, and a lack of ownership.

With this background in mind, it becomes imperative that you prioritize controlling the AI agent's identity. The moment an AI agent can act (call APIs, access data, trigger workflows), it becomes a digital actor that must be governed just like a human or service identity. Identity becomes the control plane for AI. Every user prompt, agent action, plugin invocation, and API call ultimately traces back to an identity decision somewhere in your stack. This is where Microsoft Entra must be designed

[1] Read the study at *https://onereach.ai/blog/agentic-ai-adoption-rates-roi-market-trends*.

[2] Read the study at *https://www.capgemini.com/wp-content/uploads/2025/07/Final-Web-Version-Report-AI-Agents.pdf*.

[3] Read the analysis at *https://www.reco.ai/learn/ai-agent-sprawl*.

intentionally, not as a legacy directory, but as the enforcement layer for AI trust. It is important to mention that Microsoft Entra is the suite of Identity, Security, and Governance features, while Microsoft Entra ID is the identity (directory) layer. For the purpose of this book, we will use Microsoft Entra, since there will be capabilities that expand beyond identity.

Microsoft Entra's relevance in AI security is rooted in its ability to unify humans, workloads, and emerging AI agent identities under the same Zero Trust model. AI systems do not eliminate identity risk; they amplify it. AI workloads operate at machine speed, scale automatically, and interact across trust boundaries. This changes the blast radius of identity compromise dramatically. A misused token from an AI agent is not just another risky login; it can become an automated abuse channel that moves faster than humans can react.

> **Important** From a leadership perspective, the design considerations are not purely technical. They are strategic. You are deciding how trust is established, how risk is interpreted, and how access is governed in an environment where AI systems can act independently.

Designing Microsoft Entra for AI security starts with acknowledging a fundamental shift. Identity decisions must be continuous, contextual, and adaptive. Static access controls, long-lived credentials, and coarse entitlements fail under AI-driven systems. Microsoft Entra is architected to address this through a combination of real-time identity signals, AI-driven risk evaluation, and policy enforcement via conditional access.

At a leadership level, this is not an implementation discussion; it is an architectural viewpoint. If Entra is treated as "the place where users authenticate," it will be bypassed by AI innovation. If Entra is positioned as the decision engine that mediates trust for every identity, human or non-human, it becomes foundational to AI security strategy.

Everything starts with an identity

Would you allow a human employee to operate without an identity, without accountability, and without access controls? Exactly, you wouldn't. The same approach needs to be applied to AI agents. You must think of an AI agent as a digital employee with superpowers. It can access multiple systems instantly, it can operate 24/7, it can scale actions across environments, and it can make decisions based on data. This scenario requires identity-first security.

Microsoft Entra Agent ID is a new identity type in Microsoft Entra designed specifically for AI agents. With this capability, each agent gets a unique, directory-native identity. This is a critical step because the AI agent identities participate in authentication, authorization, risk detection, governance, and conditional access. Figure 4-1 shows the core flow of how the Agent ID is created and used.

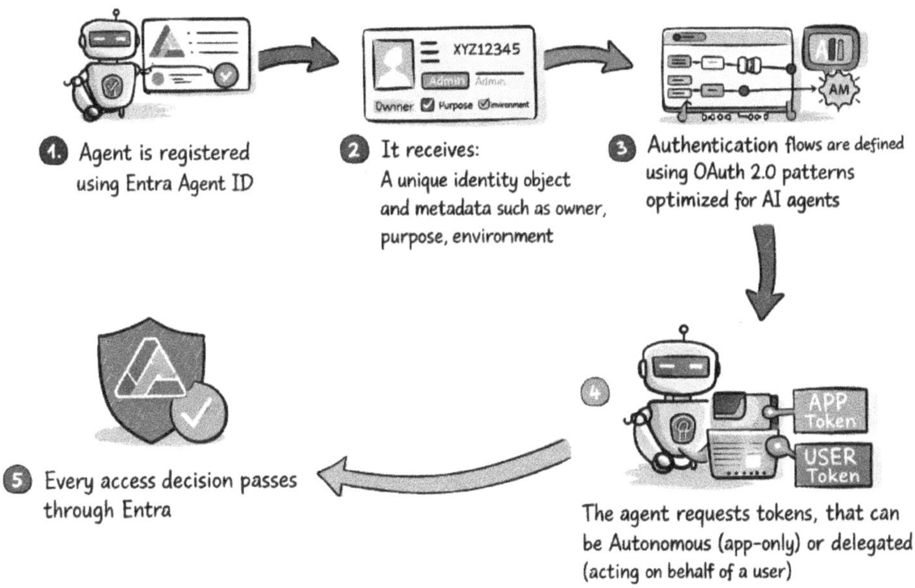

FIGURE 4-1 Agent identity lifecycle (high-level)

As you can see in Figure 4-1, Entra Agent ID builds on OAuth-based authentication, but with agent-specific semantics. First, autonomous agent identity is used when the agent acts independently. Second, agent user identity (delegated) is used when the agent acts on behalf of a user, which, in this case, maintains user attribution. Once an agent authenticates via Entra Agent ID, Microsoft Entra captures identity telemetry, including

- Authentication attempts
- Token issuance events
- Resource access attempts
- Delegation chains (user, agent)
- Conditional access evaluations

Remember the agent sprawl issue that was mentioned at the beginning of this chapter? Entra Agent ID addresses this issue by ensuring that agents don't outlive their purpose, permissions don't silently accumulate, and orphaned AI identities are avoided. Microsoft Entra Agent ID dashboard gives you a strategic overview of the agents that were identified in your tenant, including the ones that are active and unmanaged, as shown in Figure 4-2.

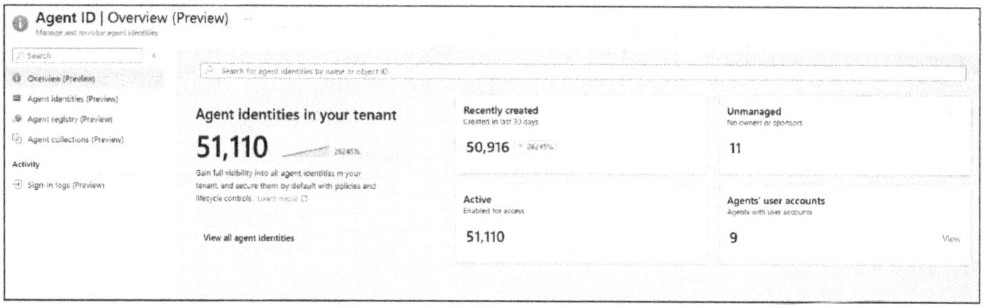

FIGURE 4-2 Agent ID dashboard

Identity signals as a foundation for Zero Trust and AI security

Zero Trust[4] is often summarized as "never trust, always verify." In practice, that principle only works if verification is driven by rich, continuously evaluated signals. AI security raises the bar further: AI systems introduce new usage patterns, new attack paths, and new identity behaviors that cannot be protected using binary allow/deny logic.

Microsoft Entra collects and correlates identity signals across multiple dimensions, as shown in Figure 4-3. For AI systems, these signals are not just useful; they are essential.

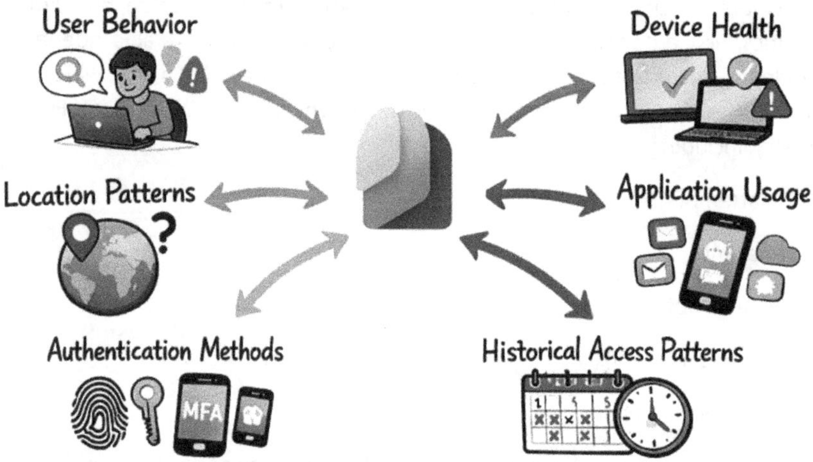

FIGURE 4-3 Identity signals

Imagine a scenario where an AI assistant is retrieving sensitive financial data for a user. Without context, that request appears legitimate. But when you layer identity signals on top, you may discover:

- The user is logging in from a new country
- The device is unmanaged

[4] In 2026, Microsoft released a new AI pillar in the Zero Trust Workshop. For more information, visit *https://www.microsoft.com/en-us/security/blog/2026/03/19/new-tools-and-guidance-announcing-zero-trust-for-ai/.*

- The request pattern is abnormal for that user
- The session originated from a risky application

This is where Microsoft Entra transforms from an identity provider into a decision intelligence platform. From a leadership standpoint, this has major implications. The first one is that you move from static access to dynamic trust. In other words, access is no longer granted once; it is continuously evaluated. In this case, every AI interaction becomes a checkpoint. This will also allow you to enable secure AI adoption at scale. Without signal-based validation, organizations often slow down AI adoption due to fear. With proper signals, you can accelerate safely.

Leaders must understand that signals are not static indicators. They are probabilistic inputs into a constant learning system. AI introduces ambiguity by design, agents operate autonomously, users interact asynchronously, and access patterns evolve quickly. Microsoft Entra's signal strategy allows organizations to shift from perimeter-based enforcement to decision-based enforcement. This matters especially when AI systems cross boundaries: internal copilots interacting with external services, developers integrating third-party models, or business users experimenting with generative AI tools. Identity signals enable Entra to evaluate risk not just at sign-in, but also at the moment of access, which is essential for Zero Trust in AI contexts.

> **Important** Conditional access for agents, which is part of the Agent ID platform, is a critical component for Zero Trust. You will learn more about this capability later in this chapter.

Microsoft Entra also provides visibility into AI-driven behavior. AI systems often operate in ways that are not immediately visible. Identity signals provide the telemetry needed to understand how AI is being used and misused. Also, it is important to mention that signals are not just for detection; they inform policy. Over time, your system becomes smarter, adapting to new patterns.

AI-powered identity protection and risk detection

When we talk about identity protection in the AI era, we need to reshape our mindset. Identity protection is no longer about stopping a stolen password. It is about containing machine-speed abuse when identity becomes execution. AI systems don't just authenticate, they act, and once identity is tied to action, compromise becomes amplification.

Microsoft Entra does not treat AI as an add-on risk or a separate control plane. It treats AI as a force multiplier of identity signals, and it applies protection accordingly, across users, workloads, and agents. Microsoft Entra ID Protection is the feature that applies to users, workloads, identities, and agents. This feature is responsible for:

- Detecting identity-based risk
- Using ML-driven baselines
- Flagging anomalous behavior over time

One important clarification is that Entra ID Protection does not inspect prompts, model output, or LLM logic. What it does observe continuously is identity behavior: for example, an AI agent suddenly accessing resources it has never used before, or an AI agent acting on behalf of a risky or compromised user. Figure 4-4 has an example of the Risky agent details page in Microsoft Entra Identity Protection, and in the Risk Evidence column, you can see more details about the agent's behavior that was flagged.

FIGURE 4-4 Risky agent details

Entra creates a baseline for an agent's normal activity and then continuously monitors it for anomalies. That baseline-vs-deviation model is the telemetry layer that gives Entra visibility into AI-driven behavior.

> **Important** For leadership, the key takeaway is that identity protection is no longer event-driven; it is narrative-driven. Entra is continuously asking, "Does this identity still behave like itself?" That's a key question for the Agentic AI era.

Most leaders are familiar with the concepts of *Risky User* and *Risky Sign-In*. What often gets missed is how these constructs evolve in AI-heavy environments. A risky sign-in is not simply a suspicious login; it is a data point in a broader behavioral story. A risky user is not just compromised; it may be on a trajectory toward compromise. AI systems amplify the importance of this distinction. In agentic scenarios, a single risky sign-in can lead to thousands of downstream actions if left unchecked. Conversely, overly aggressive responses can disrupt legitimate automation and innovation.

Risk levels (low, medium, high) are designed to inform policy decisions, not dictate them. This allows leadership teams to align risk tolerance with business criticality, especially when AI systems are involved. This allows organizations to apply stricter controls when AI identities interact with sensitive data.

Behavior-based user and sign-in risk scoring

When you begin to truly understand identity in the modern era, especially in environments infused with AI, you realize something fundamental: identity is no longer a static attribute; it is a behavior over time. The thing about behavior is, unlike credentials, it tells a story. During each sign-in, ID Protection analyzes "hundreds of signals in real time" to compute the risk level and passes it to conditional access. This is relevant for leadership because modern attackers optimize for successful sign-ins, not failed sign-ins. Risk scoring exists specifically to catch "looks valid, but feels wrong" patterns.

Microsoft Entra's approach to behavior-based user and sign-in risk scoring is rooted in this idea. It does not simply ask, *Is this the right username and password?* Instead, it asks a far more important question: *Does this activity make sense for this identity, at this moment, in this context?* Table 4-1 has an example of user risk versus sign-in risk in Microsoft Entra:

TABLE 4-1 User risk versus sign-in risk

Type of Risk Score	Types of Signals	Agentic AI Sample Scenario
User risk (likelihood that the identity itself is compromised)	■ Leaked credentials detected (dark web, breach data) ■ Unusual long-term behavior patterns ■ Confirmed compromise indicators ■ Threat intelligence correlations from Microsoft security graph ■ Risky user behavior across sessions and apps	A finance executive's credentials are exposed in a breach. An AI assistant connected to financial systems begins responding to queries initiated under that identity. Even though the queries look valid, the identity itself is compromised, meaning the AI agent could unintentionally expose sensitive financial forecasts or execute actions on behalf of an attacker.
Sign-in risk (likelihood that a specific authentication attempt is suspicious)	■ Impossible travel (geo anomalies) ■ Anonymous IP usage (TOR, VPN) ■ Malware-linked IP addresses ■ Unfamiliar device or sign-in properties ■ Token anomalies (replay, session hijack) ■ Atypical location or access timing	An AI agent acting on behalf of a user attempts to retrieve sensitive HR data. The request originates from an unfamiliar location using a TOR network. Even if the user is legitimate, this specific sign-in is flagged as high risk. Conditional access blocks the request, preventing the AI agent from executing the action under suspicious conditions.

While much of the focus is on users, the same principles apply to AI agents and workloads. Through Entra, service principals can be monitored, anomalous behavior can be detected, and access patterns can be evaluated. For example, an AI agent suddenly accesses new APIs.

> **Important** As an AI leader, behavior-based risk scoring should influence how you design your strategy.

Adaptive access with conditional access

AI agents are not passive systems; they retrieve enterprise data and execute actions across systems. In addition, they interact with APIs and act on behalf of users. With conditional access in place, AI agents only act when the conditions of trust are satisfied.

Conditional access policies enable you to define precise rules governing who can access specific resources. In addition, it allows you to establish the conditions under which access is granted and what requirements must be satisfied before access is allowed. This is applicable for human (regular use) and non-human (AI agent) identities. In the context of AI agents, this becomes especially critical. It means explicitly determining which identities, such as service principals and managed identities, are permitted to access. These capabilities ensure that AI agents operate within clearly defined and governed trust boundaries, rather than having unrestricted access to enterprise resources.

When it comes to AI agents, conditional access is no longer about whether access is allowed. It's about whether access is still aligned with intent. For human users, intent is inferred from context. For AI agents, intent is inferred from behavioral consistency. When an agent suddenly accesses unfamiliar resources or spikes token usage, conditional access becomes the tool that controls the agent.

The important thing to understand about conditional access for an AI agent is that it goes through the same workflow (Figure 4-5) as a human (user). Although they (user and agent) look different, behave differently, and authenticate differently, they converge on the same identity control plane. That convergence is intentional since Microsoft isn't trying to secure "users" and "AI" separately; it is securing identities that can act.

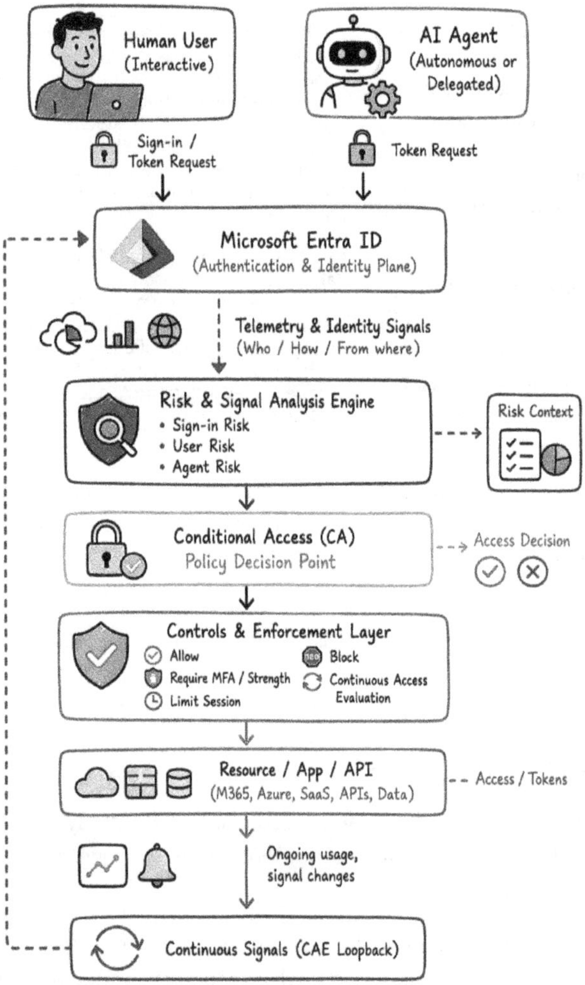

FIGURE 4-5 Human + AI agent + conditional access

Designing considerations for Microsoft Purview as your data protection solution for AI

According to a survey conducted by Glide,[5] 50 percent of businesses cite data privacy and security as the top barrier to AI adoption. In 2026, a survey from EY[6] also found that 69 percent of organizations cite AI-powered data leaks as their top concern. While these are high numbers, it makes total sense that organizations are concerned about AI adoption when the subject is data protection. AI is not just another application layer; it expands the data attack surface exponentially, requiring stronger governance, classification, and protection controls.

With this background in mind, we can also say that designing data protection with AI can't follow the same rationale as traditional systems. When you begin designing a data protection strategy for AI, you are no longer just protecting data at rest or in transit; you are protecting data in motion across reasoning systems. AI changes the game because data is continuously ingested, transformed, inferred upon, and sometimes unintentionally exposed through outputs. As a leader, this means your design approach must evolve from static controls to continuous, context-aware data protection.

Microsoft Purview provides a unified control plane across data discovery, classification, governance, and protection. But simply "turning it on" is not a strategy. The real value emerges when you deliberately design how Purview aligns with your AI architecture, whether that includes copilots, custom LLM apps, RAG pipelines, or autonomous agents.

Data security posture management (DSPM) for AI

Too many organizations begin with features instead of flows. With AI, you must invert that. It is important to understand how data moves. Figure 4-6 has an example of how data flows between data sources, AI pipelines, and outputs:

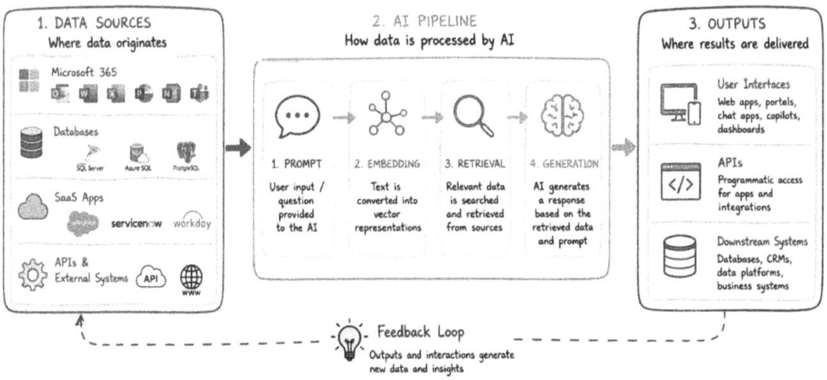

FIGURE 4-6 Data flow

[5] Read more about the state of AI in operations 2025 by Glide at *https://www.glideapps.com/ai-report-2025*.

[6] Read more about the EY survey at *https://www.ey.com/en_us/newsroom/2026/03/ey-survey-autonomous-ai-adoption-surges-at-tech-companies-as-oversight-falls-behind*.

Purview becomes foundational to give this level of visibility because it allows you to discover and map data across environments. This is critical for understanding where sensitive data might intersect with AI workloads. You also need to keep in mind that data will be queried in ways you did not anticipate, sensitive information may surface indirectly (inferred data), and outputs may combine multiple sources.

If there is one capability that leaders underestimate in AI adoption, it is visibility into data exposure risk, because at the end of the day, you cannot secure what you can't see. DSPM provides full visibility into AI apps and agents, as well as the active monitoring of shadow AI usage. From a leadership perspective, you should ensure that DSPM covers all AI-relevant data sources, not just traditional repositories. Also, make sure that exposure insights are tied to business risk (not just technical findings). These findings are actionable; make sure to integrate them into remediation workflows.

DSPM for AI is much more than just inventory; it is about understanding how your data posture changes when AI is introduced. In Purview, DSPM extends its capabilities into AI by:

- Identifying datasets used in training or grounding
- Mapping access paths that AI agents can traverse
- Highlighting over-permissioned data that could be surfaced via prompts

DSPM integrates across Endpoints, such as browser monitoring and device onboarding; Microsoft 365 services, such as SharePoint, Teams, and OneDrive; and AI platforms, such as Copilot and third-party LLMs. Figure 4-7 has an example of the data flow starting with a user interacting with AI via a prompt.

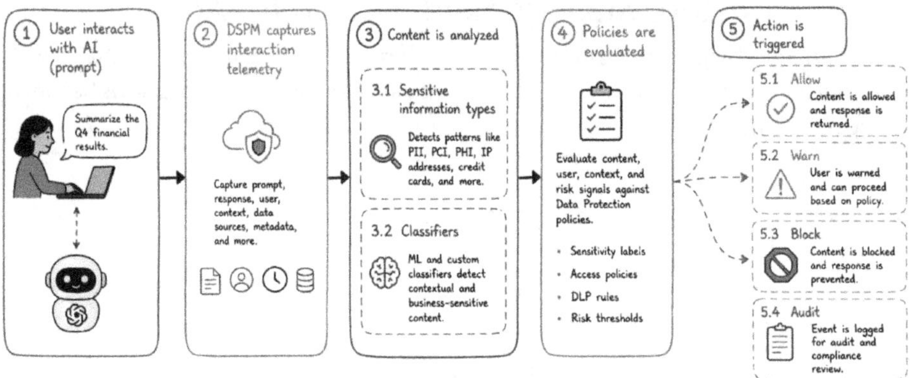

FIGURE 4-7 Data flow

As you can see, DSPM captures interaction right at the beginning of the process. DSPM becomes your "exposure radar," and without it, you are effectively deploying AI in the dark. Purview has unified data discovery across AI-relevant sources as part of DSPM capability. This discoverability applies to Microsoft 365, Azure data services, and SaaS platforms (via scanning agents). But here's the important nuance: Purview doesn't just discover data; it discovers data that AI can reach. As a leader, this means your visibility shifts from "Where is my data?" to "Where is my data exposed to AI?"

DSPM leverages classification signals such as sensitive information types (PII, financial, health data), trainable classifiers (contracts, IP, source code, internal docs), and sensitivity labels. In AI scenarios, this becomes especially powerful because you can identify which sensitive datasets are likely to surface in AI responses. In addition, you can also quantify how much of your AI-accessible data is sensitive. These signals don't just inform visibility; they also feed directly into Data Loss Prevention (DLP) policies that control how AI can interact with sensitive content.

Instead of simply listing who has access, DSPM provides a much deeper view by showing how access is granted, whether directly, through group membership, or via inherited permissions. It does that while also mapping how data flows across systems and identifying the exact paths that AI agents or users can traverse to reach sensitive information. In practice, this creates a dynamic "graph of exposure" rather than a static permissions list. For example, a sensitive document stored in SharePoint may be accessible through:

- A broadly assigned group
- Indexed and made retrievable by Microsoft 365 Copilot
- Queried by a user who only has indirect access

DSPM connects all these dots and surfaces the full chain of exposure. This level of visibility is critical for leadership because it transforms data protection from a reactive exercise into a strategic capability, enabling informed decisions about AI adoption, risk prioritization, and governance by clearly revealing how seemingly harmless configurations can lead to significant data exposure. Table 4-2 has some use case scenarios, where DSPM for AI delivers immediate value:

TABLE 4-2 Use case scenarios

Use Case	DSPM Actions	Outcome
Preparing for Microsoft 365 Copilot rollout	■ DSPM identifies overexposed Share Point sites ■ Highlights sensitive documents accessible to broad audiences ■ Recommends permission tightening	You reduce risk before AI amplifies it
Securing RAG-based applications	■ DSPM identifies datasets used for embeddings ■ Flags sensitive content in vector stores ■ Maps access paths from users to those datasets	Prevents sensitive data leakage through generated responses
Reducing insider risk in AI usage	■ DSPM reveals users with excessive access to sensitive data ■ Data that can be queried through AI tools	Enables targeted monitoring and policy enforcement
Regulatory compliance for AI	■ DSPM tracks sensitive data usage ■ Provides lineage and audit trails ■ Identify policy violations	Supports compliance with regulations (GDPR, HIPAA, etc.)

Data classification and sensitive data detection in AI

In an AI panel, during the SecOps Summit Brazil 2026, I stated that AI systems don't understand sensitivity unless you explicitly teach them what matters. The reality is, Gen AI apps and agents are incredibly capable at reasoning, summarizing, and generating, but without classification signals, they treat all data as equal. Well, that's precisely where risk begins.

The conclusion is simple: it is critical to have data classification as part of your organization's AI adoption. If you don't know what your data is, you may end up in situations where AI agents could provide sensitive data as an answer to a question. Without classification, AI governance fails immediately. In the AI era, data classification is not just labeling; it's about defining what your AI is allowed to understand, process, and generate.

This shift from static labeling to contextual intelligence is exactly where Microsoft Purview brings value. In Purview, you have Sensitive Information Types (SITs). SITs are a rich library of built-in sensitive information types, covering personally identifiable information (PII), financial data (credit cards, bank accounts), health data, and government identifiers (SSN, passport numbers). Under the hood, SITs use pattern matching (regex), keyword proximity, and checksum validation (for things like credit cards). From a technical perspective, this gives you high-confidence detection at scale. In AI scenarios, these SITs help ensure that prompts containing sensitive data are detected. It also ensures that grounding datasets are evaluated before use and outputs are inspected for potential leakage.

Another important capability in Purview is the machine learning classifiers, which analyze context, semantics, and structure. This enables the detection of contracts, source code, financial reports, and internal strategy documents. These classifiers are trained on Microsoft-curated datasets and continuously improved. This matters for AI because AI models often surface contextual data, not just structured patterns. In addition, sensitive insights may not include obvious identifiers.

Information protection for AI apps and agents

When organizations begin adopting AI at scale, one of the most common misconceptions I encounter is the assumption that if access is controlled, the data is protected. That may have been a reasonable rationale in the past, where the boundary between user, application, and data was relatively predictable. Well, AI changes that completely! AI applications and autonomous agents do not simply retrieve information; they interpret it, synthesize it, transform it, and generate new outputs based on it.

If DSPM helps you understand exposure, and classification helps AI understand sensitivity, information protection is what enforces control. It is the capability that ensures your data protection decisions remain intact even after data begins moving through AI workflows, copilots, autonomous agents, APIs, and generated outputs. From a leadership perspective, this is not merely a security feature set; it is a business control mechanism that determines whether AI can be adopted safely across the enterprise. AI introduces a dramatically different challenge, because now data can:

- Be retrieved dynamically through prompts
- Be passed between orchestrated AI agents
- Be embedded into vector databases
- Be summarized into generated responses
- Be transformed into derivative outputs
- Be copied into external systems through plugins or APIs

Let's use the scenario of a confidential board strategy document. In a traditional environment, where access is strictly limited to executives, the primary risk is direct unauthorized access. In an AI-enabled environment, however, the exposure model becomes significantly more complex. That's because that same document may be accessible through a Copilot experience, summarized by an AI agent, or consumed by another downstream agent as part of an automated workflow. In other words, now you have fragments of the content indirectly surfaced to a user through a seemingly innocent prompt, even if that user never had direct access to the original document.

In modern AI scenarios such as AI copilots, agent-based automation, document summarization workflows, and knowledge retrieval systems, information is continuously accessed, processed, and repurposed across multiple layers of interaction. Table 4-3 has some use case scenarios on how information protection helps secure the data in the AI era:

TABLE 4-3 Use case scenarios for information protection

Use Case	Scenario	Value of Information Protection	Leadership Benefit
Executive strategy document protection	A board strategy document exists in SharePoint. Without protection: Copilot may summarize it for authorized users, but derivative content may be mishandled.	With proper information protection, you can apply sensitivity labels, enforce encryption, summarize inherited classification, and block external sharing.	Strategic confidentiality is preserved.
Customer data in an AI prompt	A support employee pastes customer records into an AI assistant.	Sensitive data is detected, policy warning gets triggered, the submission is blocked, and an event is logged.	Regulatory exposure is reduced.
Autonomous procurement agent	An AI procurement agent accesses supplier contracts.	With protection, you can apply confidentiality labels, restrict the agent to approved repositories, and govern the output sharing.	Automation without uncontrolled data leakage.

Leaders will face many decisions to make when it comes to information protection for AI apps and agents. Figure 4-8 highlights the top five decisions to make in this scope of information protection.

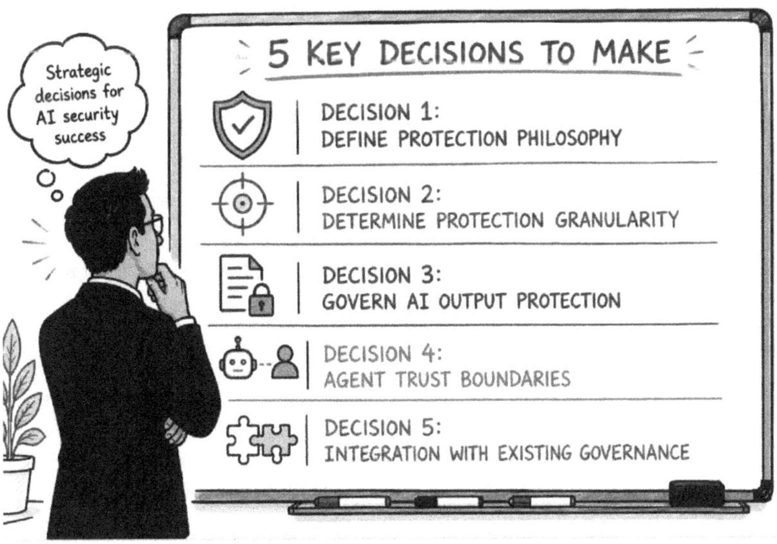

FIGURE 4-8 Strategic information protection decisions for leaders

The first strategic decision is about its operating philosophy. Should AI be open by default, with restrictions applied only to exceptions, or should it be restrictive by default, enabling only explicitly approved scenarios? The answer will vary depending on the organization's risk appetite, regulatory obligations, and innovation objectives. Highly regulated industries such as finance, healthcare, and government often lean toward restrictive models to minimize exposure and maintain tighter control, while innovation-driven organizations may prefer a more progressive enablement approach to accelerate experimentation and business transformation. Neither model is inherently right or wrong, but what matters most is that this choice is made deliberately, with clear alignment to business priorities, governance expectations, and the organization's broader AI strategy.

The second decision is determining the right level of protection granularity, because both extremes create significant challenges for the organization. If controls are too coarse, everything may be labeled as confidential, which can create unnecessary friction, reduce employee productivity, and ultimately diminish the practical value of AI by making access to useful information overly restrictive. On the other hand, if protections are too loose, sensitive content may be inadvertently exposed, governance controls may lose effectiveness, and the organization's overall risk posture can weaken. Leadership must carefully calibrate this balance, ensuring that protections are precise enough to safeguard critical information without unnecessarily slowing innovation or limiting AI's business impact.

The third decision is governing how AI-generated content should be protected. This is a question that many organizations initially overlook, but that becomes critically important as AI adoption matures. Leadership must decide whether content created, transformed, or summarized by AI should inherit the same protection controls as the original source material. For example, if an AI system summarizes an executive strategy document that is highly confidential, should that generated summary be treated with the same level of protection? In most organizations, the answer should be yes, because while the format of the content has changed, the sensitivity of the underlying information has not. This requires intentional policy design to ensure that protection follows not only the original data, but also the derivative intelligence AI creates from it.

The fourth decision is establishing trust boundaries for AI agents, recognizing that not all agents should be granted the same level of access or operational freedom. An internal HR agent handling employee records, a finance reporting agent processing sensitive business metrics, a customer-facing chatbot interacting with external users, and a third-party plugin agent integrated into your environment each present very different risk profiles and trust assumptions. Treating them all equally would create unnecessary exposure and weaken governance. Protection policies should intentionally reflect these trust differences, defining clear boundaries around what each type of agent can access, process, generate, and share, ensuring that autonomy is granted proportionally to the level of trust and business necessity.

The last decision is to ensure that AI adoption is fully integrated with the organization's existing governance and protection frameworks. This becomes particularly important in high-value scenarios such as engineering teams using AI copilots to accelerate development. While these tools can significantly improve productivity and innovation, they also introduce the risk of exposing proprietary source code, architectural designs, or other intellectual property. To mitigate this, organizations should implement controls such as source code classifiers to identify sensitive development assets, automatic labeling to ensure consistent protection, data loss prevention policies to prevent unauthorized sharing or exfiltration, and restricted sharing controls that limit where protected code can be used or transmitted. For leadership, the strategic benefit is clear: enabling engineering innovation and AI-assisted productivity without compromising the intellectual property that differentiates the business.

Data governance for AI

When most leaders hear the term *data governance*, they immediately think about compliance, policies, regulatory requirements, and controls. While those elements are certainly important, AI has fundamentally changed the role governance plays within the organization. Governance is no longer simply about controlling data; it is about creating the trust framework that allows AI to operate responsibly, safely, and at scale.

One of the observations I frequently share with executives is that organizations rarely fail in their AI initiatives because of model quality. More often, they struggle because they cannot answer basic governance questions: *What data is being used? Where did it come from? Who owns it? Can we trust it? Should AI have access to it?* Without clear answers, AI quickly becomes a source of uncertainty rather than a driver of business value, as shown in Figure 4-9.

FIGURE 4-9 Governance questions that must be answered

Traditional applications typically interact with well-defined datasets and business processes. But AI systems are different. An AI application may retrieve information from multiple repositories simultaneously, combine structured and unstructured data, and generate conclusions based on information from multiple business units.

When I think about AI governance, I encourage leadership teams to think beyond compliance and focus on four strategic questions: *What data do we have? Where did it come from? Who owns it? Should AI be allowed to use it?* Governance ensures that AI is built upon data that is discoverable, understandable, trustworthy, and accountable.

Microsoft Purview enables AI governance by providing end-to-end visibility, classification, control, and compliance over enterprise data, ensuring that AI systems are built on trusted, secure, and policy-compliant datasets. This directly reduces risk in Gen AI scenarios (e.g., data leakage, bias from ungoverned data, regulatory violations) while accelerating safe AI adoption. Table 4-4 has the mapping of governance needs and purview capabilities:

TABLE 4-4 Governance needs and Purview capabilities

Governance Need	Purview Capability	This Feature Helps to Answer the Question	Key Supporting Features
Discover and understand the AI data estate	Data map and unified catalog	What data do we have, and where is it located across the organization?	Data Map (automated scanning, metadata capture), Unified Catalog (searchable inventory), Business glossary, and data catalog search.
Make data discoverable and usable for AI	Data catalog and data governance domains	How can data consumers and AI builders find trusted, approved datasets?	Catalog search, metadata enrichment, governance domains, data products, stewardship, and ownership assignment.
Classify and protect sensitive data used by AI	Information Protection and data classification	Is this data sensitive, and how should it be handled when used in AI?	Sensitivity labels, auto-classification (built-in classifiers), custom classifiers, and label inheritance across systems.
Prevent data leakage and control AI access	Data loss prevention (DLP) and data policies	How do we prevent sensitive data from being exposed through AI or shared inappropriately?	DLP policies, endpoint DLP, enforcement and audit modes, Data Policy controls, integration with Copilot and AI apps.
Establish trust and traceability of AI data	Data lineage	Where did this data come from, and how has it been transformed before being used in AI?	End-to-end lineage tracking, visualization of upstream/downstream dependencies, integration with pipelines and analytics systems.
Ensure data quality and reliability for AI outputs	Data estate insights/metadata intelligence	Can we trust the quality and consistency of the data feeding AI models?	Metadata insights, impact analysis, observability of data flows, and dependency tracking.
Control access and enforce governance policies	Access control and governance model (RBAC, domains)	Who has access to this data, and are they allowed to use it in AI scenarios? [intradyn.com]	Role-based access control (RBAC), governance domains, collections, delegated ownership, and policy enforcement.
Identify and reduce data exposure risks in an AI scenario	Data security posture management (DSPM)	Where is sensitive data overexposed or at risk of being accessed by AI systems?	DSPM for data, risk visibility, policy recommendations, and monitoring of AI and data interactions.

If you step back and look at this table holistically, what Purview is really giving you is a way to shift AI governance from reactive to proactive. Instead of waiting for issues like data leakage, compliance gaps, or untrusted outputs, you now have a structured way to answer the foundational questions before data ever reaches an AI model. That's the mindset shift I'd encourage you to anchor on with leadership: governance isn't a blocker to AI innovation; it's the enabler that makes AI trustworthy and scalable. The organizations that get this right are the ones treating data governance as part of their AI architecture, not as an afterthought layered on top.

From a leadership perspective, there are a few practical tips worth keeping in mind. First, prioritize visibility before control. If you don't have a clear inventory of your data estate, any AI governance conversation will be incomplete. Second, standardize classification early, especially for sensitive data, because everything downstream (DLP, access control, Copilot safety) depends on it. Third, treat lineage as a business requirement, not just a technical feature. It becomes essential when you need to explain AI decisions to regulators, customers, or even your own executives. And finally, drive cross-functional ownership: governance is not just a security or IT responsibility. Data owners, AI teams, compliance, and business stakeholders all need to align on how data is used in AI scenarios. If you can operationalize that alignment, Purview becomes much more than a tool; it becomes the control plane for responsible AI in your organization.

Designing considerations for Microsoft Defender for Cloud as your cloud security solution for AI

Up until now in this chapter, some essential areas of securing AI were covered, including data protection, identity, and governance for AI. Those are all essential. However, there is another reality that becomes increasingly important as AI deployments mature: AI workloads themselves become part of your attack surface.

When I speak with CISOs, security architects, and executive leadership teams, I often emphasize that AI security should be approached through two complementary lenses:

- AI Security Posture Management (AI-SPM): understanding and reducing AI risk before compromise occurs.
- AI Threat Protection: detecting and responding when attacks target AI systems.

You can think of AI-SPM as preventing misconfigurations, excessive exposure, and weak governance. AI Threat Protection is the capacity to rapidly identify adversaries that are attempting to exploit those weaknesses. AI-SPM addresses the question: *"How do we know whether our AI environment is secure before attackers find weaknesses?"* while AI Threat Protection addresses the question, *"Is there any threat actor attacking my AI workloads?"*

> **Important** Organizations will not secure AI through threat detection alone, and they will not secure AI through posture management alone. They need both.

Most AI-related security incidents do not begin with sophisticated attackers. They begin with the exposure of excessive permissions, publicly exposed endpoints, insecure AI plugins, misconfigured model deployments, or overprivileged AI agents. In other words, exposure precedes exploitation. This is why posture management is so important. If organizations can identify exposure before attackers discover it, they dramatically reduce risk. Figure 4-10 has a visual representation of the common exposures and the importance of AI-SPM.

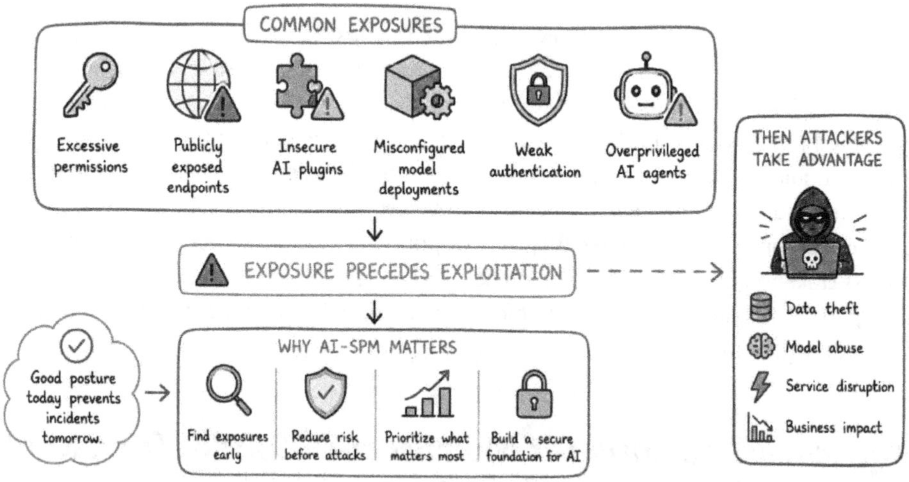

FIGURE 4-10 The importance of AI-SPM

Risk prioritization and contextual security recommendations

Microsoft Defender for Cloud provides discoverability, which is super important, because you can't protect against what you don't know exists, and the visibility across AI services deployed in an Azure environment. Once discovered and visible, Defender for Cloud, more specifically a paid plan for Defender Cloud Security Posture Management (DCSPM), will evaluate the security state of those AI services and provide recommendations to improve the security posture of those workloads. Defender for Cloud continuously discovers AI-related resources, including

- Azure OpenAI
- Microsoft Foundry
- Azure Machine Learning
- Amazon Bedrock
- Gemini Enterprise Agent Platform (formerly Vertex AI)
- Model endpoints
- Gen AI apps

This creates a centralized inventory of AI assets. For leadership, this provides something incredibly valuable, as it creates a complete picture of the organization's AI footprint. As part of this process,

Defender CSPM also collects insights (misconfigurations, over-permissioned identities, vulnerabilities, and data exposure) across all supported assets and creates the attack path, which shows how an attacker could move through your AI environment. This is incredibly important for prioritization.

But remember, not all risks are equal, and AI-SPM helps you focus on the ones that are exploitable. Defender for Cloud consolidates risks and integrates them into Secure Score, which can be used to track the progress of an AI workload's security improvement over time. Risk prioritization is done by looking at different variables, such as Internet exposure, possibility of lateral movement, and vulnerability level. By using risk factors to rank security recommendations, Defender for Cloud enables organizations to transform security into a measurable and trackable discipline rather than treating it solely as an operational concern. Figure 4-11 has an example of the Defender for Cloud dashboard showing the Secure Score by workload.

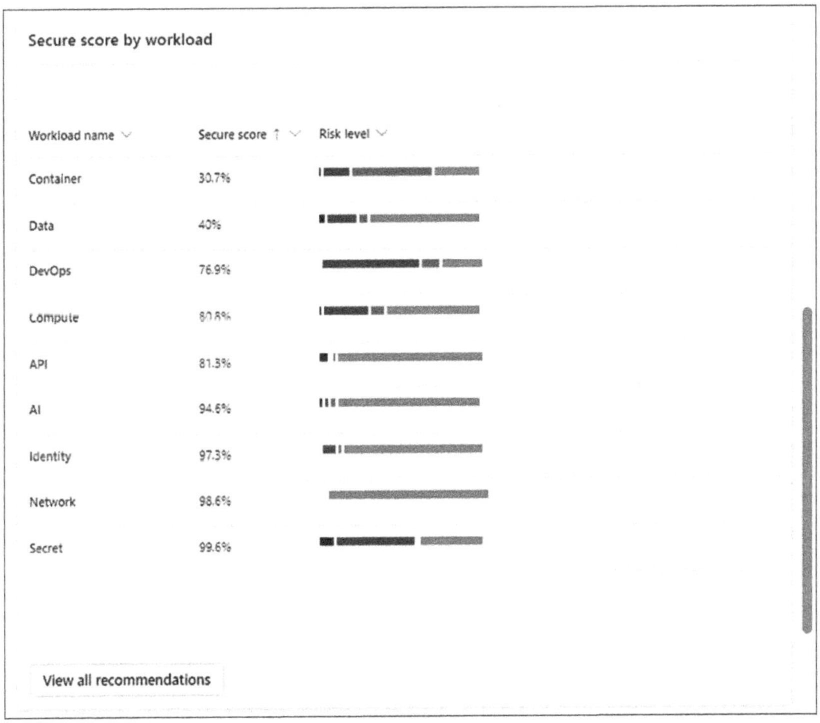

FIGURE 4-11 Breakdown of Secure Score per workload

Is very important for you to consider how you operationalize risk prioritization and governance at scale. AI-SPM generates a large volume of insights, from misconfigurations to potential attack paths, and as described previously, not all of them matter equally. This is where leaders must intentionally design for context-driven prioritization, leveraging capabilities like attack path analysis and risk-based scoring to focus teams on what is truly exploitable. Technically, this means tuning policies, integrating with identity and access governance, and aligning recommendations with your broader cloud security baseline. Strategically, however, this is about accountability: assigning ownership for remediation, embedding security into DevOps workflows, and ensuring that posture improvements are measurable over time. The organizations that succeed are the ones that treat AI security posture not as a static report, but as a continuous, governed process tied to business risk.

As you think about operationalizing AI-SPM with Defender for Cloud, Table 4-5 has some common questions I would expect strong leaders to ask themselves and their teams, and how Defender for Cloud can help:

TABLE 4-5 Strategic questions to ask about AI-SPM operationalization

Leadership Question	Defender for Cloud Capability
Do we have a complete and continuously updated inventory of all AI assets across our environment?	AI BOM (AI Bill of Materials) discovery and continuous multi-cloud AI workload inventory
Can we clearly understand how data flows through our AI systems and where sensitive data is exposed?	Data-aware AI posture insights and asset/context discovery across models, datasets, and integrations
Are we able to prioritize AI risks based on actual exploitability rather than the volume of findings?	Attack path analysis and risk-based prioritization with contextual exposure management
How do we ensure accountability for remediating AI-related risks across engineering and security teams?	Governance workflows, ownership assignment, and remediation tracking within Defender CSPM
Are we embedding AI security controls early enough in the development lifecycle to prevent issues before deployment?	Defender CSPM DevSecOps integration with IaC scanning, code repository analysis, and pipeline security checks
Do we have visibility into misconfigurations and vulnerabilities across both code and cloud layers of AI workloads?	Unified posture visibility across code-to-cloud, including vulnerability scanning and configuration assessment
Can we map potential attack paths that an attacker could use to compromise our AI systems?	Cloud Security Explorer and AI-specific attack path analysis capabilities
How do we measure improvement in our AI security posture over time at an executive level?	Secure Score, risk dashboards, and posture tracking metrics within Defender for Cloud

Threat protection for AI workloads

Now let's shift from posture to runtime, because even with the best posture in place, attackers will still try to exploit your AI systems. This is particularly important when you are using a Zero Trust approach, where assume breach is one of the principles. In other words, you need to assume that AI workloads will be attacked, and you need to detect and respond fast. To detect, you need to have quality-level analytics that can identify a wide range of attacks against your AI workloads.

Traditional cloud security is largely about detecting known patterns, malware, suspicious logins, and lateral movement, but AI introduces an entirely new layer where the attack surface lives inside the interaction itself. Defender for Cloud approaches this by analyzing both prompts and model responses, looking for signals that indicate something is off, whether that be attempts to bypass safeguards, extract sensitive information, or manipulate system behavior. It's not just looking for known bad signatures; it's trying to understand intent, context, and behavior, which is exactly what makes securing generative AI fundamentally different.

One of the most important aspects of how Microsoft approaches this problem is the alignment with the OWASP Top 10 for LLM applications. Instead of treating AI threats as abstract risks, Defender for

Cloud maps its detection logic to concrete categories like prompt injection, sensitive data disclosure, data poisoning, and improper output handling. This gives security teams a structured way to reason about AI risk while also enabling consistent analytics. For example, a prompt injection attempt, where a user tries to override system instructions, can be identified by analyzing both the content and the deviation from expected patterns. Similarly, detections around sensitive information disclosure look for cases where the model may expose secrets or regulated data, while supply chain or model integrity risks focus on anomalies in dependencies or model behavior. This mapping ensures that what you're detecting is not just technically valid but also aligned with industry-recognized threat models.

Another key design element, and something I always emphasize to leaders, is how Defender for Cloud brings together multiple signals to increase fidelity. It integrates deeply with Microsoft Foundry Content Safety, which provides real-time filtering and blocking of harmful or unsafe content, including prompt injections and malicious inputs. Those signals are not isolated; they are enriched with Microsoft threat intelligence and correlated with activity across identities, infrastructure, and applications. The result is a much richer, contextual alert that tells you not just that something happened, but why it matters and what it might be connected to. And when these detections flow into Defender XDR, they become part of a broader incident, enabling security teams to investigate and respond holistically. Figure 4-12 has a visual representation of this flow.

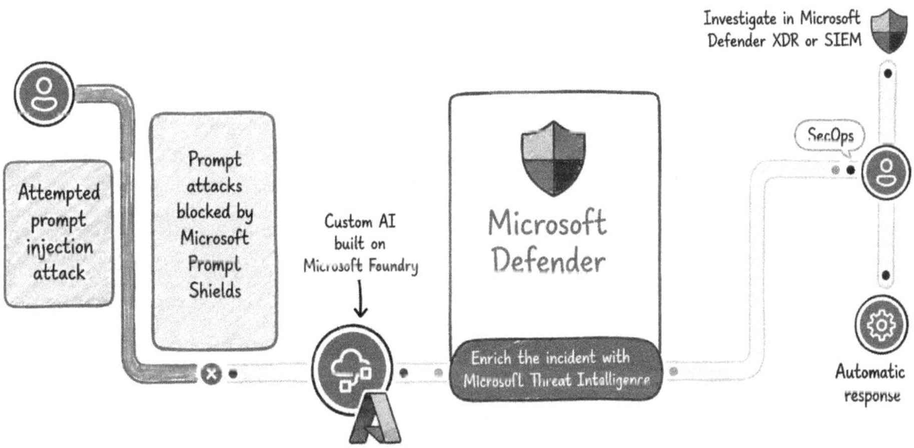

FIGURE 4-12 Threat protection workflow in Defender for Cloud

Figure 4-12 is a classic example of Microsoft Foundry Content Safety prompt shields integration with Defender for Cloud, particularly Defender for AI Services, which is the paid plan. Table 4-6 has some other sample scenarios where these two services will complement each other:

TABLE 4-6 Integration between Azure AI Content Safety and Defender for AI Services

Type of Attack	AI Service Responsible for the Detection	Which Feature Detects It, and How Are Features
Jailbreak/direct prompt injection attempt	Microsoft Foundry Content Safety/Prompt Shields	Prompt Shields detects attempts to manipulate or bypass the system prompt and model safeguards; in the blocked scenario, the prompt is stopped in real time. Microsoft Defender for Cloud can notify the SOC when a jailbreak attempt is blocked by Microsoft Foundry Content Safety Prompt Shields. This is a strong "better together" case: Prompt Shields blocks or detects the prompt attack, while Defender for AI Services turns that signal into a contextual security alert for investigation.
ASCII smuggling/encoded prompt injection	Defender for AI Services	Defender for AI Services detects encoded manipulation techniques, such as ASCII smuggling and prompt injection, where attackers try to hide malicious instructions using encodings to bypass controls. This complements Microsoft Foundry Content Safety / Prompt Shields because Prompt Shields focuses on adversarial prompt detection and blocking, while Defender for AI Services adds SOC-facing alerting, evidence, and correlation for investigation.
Sensitive data exposure/data exfiltration through prompts or responses	Defender for AI Services	Defender for AI Services detects suspicious exposure of sensitive data, including anomalies where sensitive information is exposed by an AI resource, and can provide contextual alerts with supporting evidence, such as sensitive information types or credentials accessed. This complements Microsoft Foundry Content Safety because content filtering can help reduce unsafe outputs, while Defender for AI Services gives SecOps visibility into whether sensitive data exposure is part of a broader attack chain.
Malicious or phishing URL surfaced through an AI application	Defender for AI Services	Defender for AI Services detects malicious URL scenarios, such as a phishing URL shared in an AI application or a corrupted AI application/model/data directing a phishing attempt at a user. This complements Microsoft Foundry Content Safety / Prompt Shields because Prompt Shields can help stop prompt attacks at input time, while Defender for AI Services detects malicious outcomes in the AI conversation and enriches them with threat intelligence and application context for SOC investigation.

As you extend your thinking beyond traditional generative AI workloads, Agentic AI introduces a new set of dynamics that fundamentally changes the threat model, and Defender for Cloud is evolving accordingly to address this. Unlike static AI applications, agents are designed to take actions: they call APIs, interact with external systems, retrieve and manipulate data, and in some cases, even orchestrate multi-step workflows with minimal human intervention. This creates an expanded attack surface where the risk is no longer limited to what the model says, but what the system does. Defender for Cloud detects these risks by monitoring agent behaviors, tool interactions, and execution patterns, looking for anomalies such as unauthorized tool calls, unexpected privilege escalation, or abnormal chaining of actions. The challenge here is not just detecting malicious input but identifying when an agent is being coerced into doing something it was technically allowed to do but shouldn't have done in that context.

What makes Agentic AI particularly sensitive is the notion of delegated trust and autonomy. When you give an agent access to systems, whether that's retrieving data from a knowledge base, invoking a function, or triggering an external workflow, you're essentially extending your security boundary. This introduces new risks like excessive agency, tool misuse, and lateral movement across integrated systems. Defender for Cloud addresses this by combining runtime behavior analytics, identity context, and threat intelligence, allowing it to detect when an agent is operating outside of expected patterns or interacting with systems in suspicious ways. For example, an agent repeatedly querying sensitive data sources, or invoking tools in a sequence that resembles reconnaissance or data exfiltration behavior, can trigger alerts even if each individual action appears valid. Figure 4-13 has an example of these different Agentic AI interactions and the proper guardrails for each scenario.

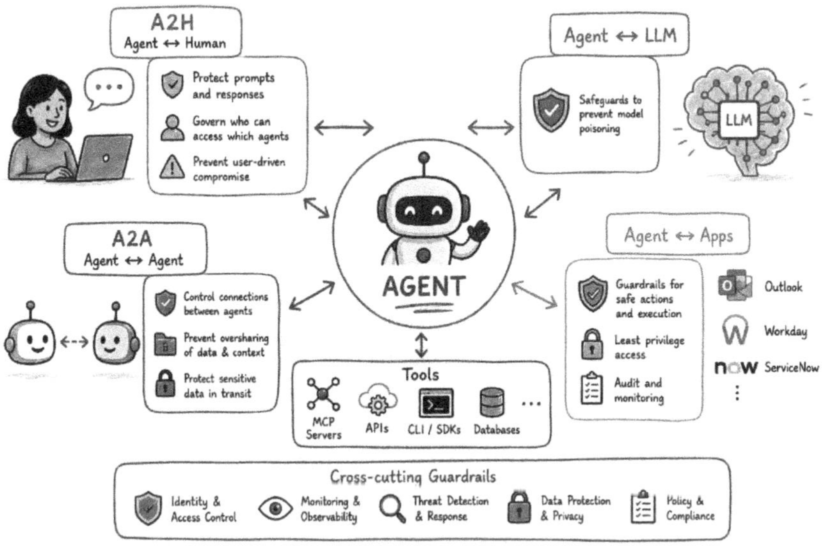

FIGURE 4-13 Risks introduced by Agentic AI and the recommended guardrails

As a leader, this is where your strategy needs to evolve: it's not just about securing models anymore; it's about governing autonomous decision-making systems, ensuring that as agents become more capable, they don't unintentionally become powerful attack vectors within your environment. I often tell executives that AI threat protection should not be viewed solely as a cybersecurity capability; it is fundamentally a business resilience capability. The reason is simple: AI is rapidly becoming embedded in the very fabric of modern organizations, influencing customer experiences, enhancing employee productivity, supporting decision-making processes, and driving critical business operations.

As organizations become increasingly dependent on AI to deliver services, generate insights, and automate workflows, the impact of a successful attack extends far beyond the technology itself. An attack against an AI system can disrupt business processes, erode customer trust, impair decision-making, and directly affect revenue and operational continuity. In many organizations today, protecting AI is no longer just about securing a technology platform; it is about protecting the business functions that increasingly depend on it. As AI adoption grows, leadership should regularly ask:

- Which AI systems are most critical?
- How are we monitoring them?
- How quickly can we detect attacks?

- What AI-specific detections do we have?
- Are AI incidents included in our response plans?
- Can we quantify AI risk exposure?

Ultimately, the organizations that will succeed with AI are not necessarily the ones deploying the largest models or building the most sophisticated agents, but the ones that establish the strongest foundation of security, governance, and operational resilience around them. AI Security Posture Management and AI Threat Protection provide the visibility and protection needed to understand risk before an incident occurs and to respond effectively when threats emerge. Together, they enable leaders to move beyond reactive security and adopt a proactive approach that continuously measures exposure, validates controls, and protects critical AI-driven business processes.

Next steps

In this chapter, we explored how to design identity, data, and cloud security controls for AI solutions using Microsoft Entra, Microsoft Purview, and Microsoft Defender for Cloud. The chapter emphasized that AI systems, especially agents, expand the security boundary because they can act on behalf of users, access sensitive data, call APIs, and operate across cloud and enterprise environments. To adopt AI safely, organizations must treat identity as the trust control plane, data protection as a continuous governance discipline, and cloud security as a combination of posture management and runtime threat protection.

- **Designing considerations for Microsoft Entra as your identity security solution for AI:** Microsoft Entra provides the identity foundation for AI security by governing human users, workloads, and AI agents through Zero Trust principles, continuous risk evaluation, and policy-based access control.
- **Everything starts with an identity:** AI agents must be treated as governed digital actors, with unique identities, authentication, authorization, telemetry, and lifecycle controls through Microsoft Entra Agent ID.
- **Identity signals as a foundation for Zero Trust and AI security:** Identity signals such as location, device state, behavioral patterns, and risky applications enable Microsoft Entra to make dynamic trust decisions for AI interactions.
- **AI-powered identity protection and risk detection:** Microsoft Entra ID Protection uses identity behavior, risk signals, and anomaly detection to identify compromised users, risky sign-ins, and abnormal AI agent activity.
- **Behavior-based user and sign-in risk scoring:** User risk and sign-in risk help organizations detect suspicious identity behavior over time and apply controls before compromised identities can amplify AI-driven actions.

- **Adaptive access with conditional access:** Conditional access ensures that users and AI agents can act only when the conditions of trust are satisfied, aligning access decisions with intent, behavior, and business risk.
- **Designing considerations for Microsoft Purview as your data protection solution for AI:** Microsoft Purview helps organizations protect AI-accessible data through discovery, classification, governance, information protection, and policy enforcement.
- **Data security posture management (DSPM) for AI:** DSPM provides visibility into AI-accessible data, overexposed repositories, access paths, shadow AI usage, and sensitive datasets that could be surfaced through AI systems.
- **Data classification and sensitive data detection in AI:** Data classification and sensitive information detection teach AI systems where boundaries exist, helping prevent sensitive data from being exposed through prompts, grounding data, or generated outputs.
- **Information protection for AI apps and agents:** Information protection applies to labels, encryption, restrictions, monitoring, and governance, so protection follows data as it moves through copilots, agents, APIs, and AI-generated outputs.
- **Data governance for AI:** Data governance establishes the trust framework for responsible AI by answering what data exists, where it came from, who owns it, whether it can be trusted, and whether AI should use it.
- **Designing considerations for Microsoft Defender for Cloud as your cloud security solution for AI:** Microsoft Defender for Cloud secures AI workloads by combining AI Security Posture Management with AI Threat Protection across cloud, model, application, and agent environments.
- **Risk prioritization and contextual security recommendations:** Defender for Cloud discovers AI assets, evaluates posture, identifies attack paths, prioritizes exploitable risks, and helps leaders track remediation through Secure Score and governance workflows.
- **Threat protection for AI workloads:** Defender for Cloud detects and responds to AI-specific attacks such as prompt injection, sensitive data exposure, malicious URLs, encoded manipulation, and suspicious agent behavior by correlating runtime signals with threat intelligence.

APPENDIX A

Preparing for AI Transformation Leader Exam (AB-731)

"Preparation is the key to success."

Alexander Graham Bell

IN THIS APPENDIX, YOU WILL:

- Understand how this book maps the topics covered in the Exam AB-731
- Develop the mindset to prepare for Exam AB-731

How to use this book to study for AB-731

Preparing for AB-731 means that you need to understand how organizations can take advantage of AI to drive meaningful transformation. That includes recognizing where AI can create value, choosing the right tools and resources, planning for successful adoption, improving business processes, and fostering innovation through solutions such as Microsoft 365 Copilot and Microsoft Foundry services.

This certification is intended for business leaders, managers, and decision-makers who are helping their teams or organizations navigate change and embrace new technologies. While you won't be expected to write code, you should be comfortable discussing AI capabilities, understanding their business impact, and helping guide AI initiatives across different teams and functions. To be successful in this area, you should be able to identify opportunities where AI can make a difference, promote responsible and ethical AI practices, and ensure that AI investments support broader business objectives. Experience with organizational change management and technology adoption is also valuable. In addition, you should have a working knowledge of Microsoft 365 services, Microsoft Foundry, and the core concepts and capabilities of modern AI solutions. Figure A-1 has a summary of the topics covered on this exam.

The exam outline[1] (based on the date that this appendix was written) shown in Table A-1, has the breakdown of topics and how it maps to each chapter of this book:

[1] For the latest outline, always use the online version at *https://learn.microsoft.com/en-us/credentials/certifications/resources/study-guides/ab-731*.

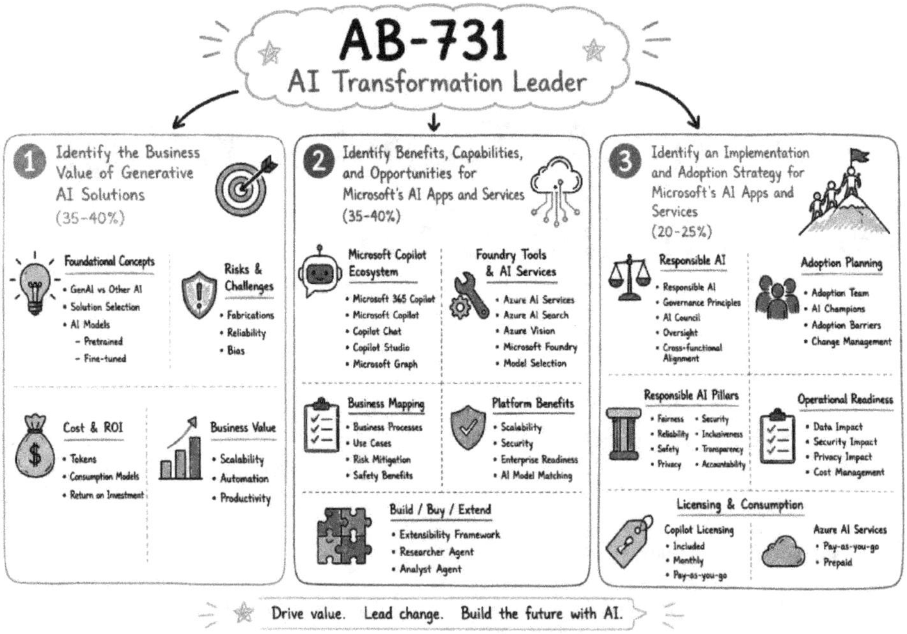

FIGURE A-1 Summary of the AB-731 Exam

TABLE A-1 Exam topics and how they map to the book

Exam Area and Percentage	Topics Covered	Chapter of This Book That Covers These Topics
Identify the business value of generative AI solutions (35–40 percent)	Identify the foundational concepts of generative AI ■ Describe the differences between generative AI and other types of AI ■ Select a generative AI solution to meet a business need ■ Describe the differences between AI models, including fine-tuned and pretrained models ■ Explain the cost drivers in generative AI usage, including tokens and return-on-investment (ROI) considerations ■ Identify the challenges of using generative AI solutions, including fabrications, reliability, and bias ■ Identify when generative AI solutions can provide business value, including scalability and automation Identify the benefits and capabilities of generative AI solutions ■ Describe the impact of prompt engineering ■ Understand techniques of prompt engineering ■ Identify business requirements for grounding solutions ■ Understand how retrieval-augmented generation (RAG) is used for AI solutions ■ Understand the impact of data on AI solutions, including data type, data quality, and representative data sets ■ Describe the importance of secure AI ■ Identify scenarios when machine learning adds value	1

Exam Area and Percentage	Topics Covered	Chapter of This Book That Covers These Topics
	■ Describe the lifecycle of a machine learning solution ■ Identify security considerations for AI systems, including application security,* data security, and authentication requirements	
Identify benefits, capabilities, and opportunities for Microsoft's AI apps and services (35–40 percent)	Identify the benefits and capabilities of Microsoft 365 Copilot and Microsoft Copilot ■ Map business processes and use cases to Copilot ■ Understand differences in capabilities between versions of Copilot ■ Understand the capabilities of Microsoft 365 Copilot Chat web and mobile experiences ■ Understand the capabilities of the Copilot experience in various Microsoft 365 apps ■ Understand the capabilities of Microsoft Copilot Studio ■ Understand the capabilities of Microsoft Graph ■ Identify benefits and capabilities of an integrated Microsoft AI solution, including risk mitigation and safety benefits ■ Map business processes and use cases to Microsoft's AI apps and services ■ Identify when to use Researcher or Analyst in Copilot ■ Identify when to build, buy, or extend, including the Microsoft 365 Copilot extensibility framework Identify the benefits and capabilities of Foundry Tools ■ Map business processes and use cases to Foundry Tools ■ Identify capabilities of Microsoft Foundry services, including Azure Vision in Foundry Tools, Foundry IQ, and Microsoft Foundry ■ Match an AI model to a business need ■ Identify the benefits of Microsoft Foundry and Foundry Tools, including scalability and security*	2
Identify an implementation and adoption strategy for Microsoft's AI apps and services (20–25 percent)	Align an AI strategy with Microsoft's responsible AI policies ■ Explain the importance of responsible AI ■ Establish governance principles for AI use ■ Establish an AI council to guide strategy, oversight, and cross-functional alignment ■ Ensure that AI solutions meet responsible AI standards, including fairness, reliability, safety, privacy, security, inclusiveness, transparency, and accountability Align an AI strategy with Microsoft's responsible AI policies ■ Establish an adoption team ■ Identify common barriers to adoption ■ Establish an AI Champions program ■ Understand potential impacts to data, security, privacy, and cost ■ Understand Copilot license types, including pay-as-you-go, monthly, and included with a Microsoft 365 subscription ■ Understand Azure AI services subscription models, including pay-as-you-go and prepaid	3

** All security-related topics are aggregated in Chapter 4. Keep in mind that Chapter 4 of this book covers way more content than the exam AB-731. In other words, you don't need to study the entire content of Chapter 4.*

The mindset to prepare for Exam AB-731

One of the most important mindset shifts that you must have (mainly if you are a technical person) is that AB-731 is fundamentally a leadership exam. It evaluates your ability to think like someone responsible for guiding AI transformation within an organization. In other words, Microsoft is not asking whether you can build an AI model. Microsoft is asking whether you can recognize where AI creates business value, understand the risks involved, help your organization adopt AI responsibly, and make informed decisions about AI investments.

As you prepare for this certification, imagine yourself sitting at a conference room table with executives from finance, operations, security, legal, and human resources. The discussion is not about prompts, Python code, or model architecture. The discussion is about solving business problems, reducing costs, increasing productivity, improving customer experience, and enabling innovation. That is the mindset you need throughout your preparation.

Understanding your role as an AI transformation leader

An AI transformation leader serves as the bridge between technology and business outcomes. In summary, there is no expectation that you will be a data scientist or a machine learning engineer. Instead, you are expected to answer questions such as:

- Where can AI create measurable value?
- Which business processes should be prioritized?
- What are the risks of adoption?
- How should we govern AI usage?
- Which Microsoft AI solution best fits the business need?
- How do we ensure responsible AI implementation?
- How do we measure success?

As you read each chapter of this book in preparation for the exam, try to reflect on a simple question: "What business problem is being solved?" By creating the habit of thinking this way, you can go to the exam with this mindset, and this simple question can help eliminate incorrect answers during the exam.

Many technology professionals naturally gravitate toward technical details. The AB-731 exam requires a different perspective. Imagine a company struggling with employee productivity. A technical thinker might ask: *What model should we use?* An AI transformation leader asks: *Why are employees losing productivity in the first place?*

The second question, asked by the AI transformation leader, will dig into the root of the problem, which can be:

- Excessive time spent searching for information
- Manual report generation

- Repetitive administrative tasks
- Slow decision-making processes

Once the problem is understood, AI solutions become easier to identify. The exam frequently tests your ability to connect business challenges with AI opportunities. Table A-2 shows the four pillar questions behind most exam scenarios:

TABLE A-2 Pillar questions

Question	Considerations	Additional Tips
Does AI create business value?	The first thing an AI transformation leader evaluates is value. Potential benefits include increased productivity, reduced operational costs, improved customer satisfaction, and faster decision-making. If an AI initiative does not create measurable business value, it becomes difficult to justify investment.	During the exam, the correct answer is often the option that provides the strongest business outcome rather than the most advanced technology.
Is it responsible?	Responsible AI is a recurring theme throughout the certification. Every AI initiative should be evaluated against these principles.[2]	Whenever you see exam questions discussing governance, ethics, bias, privacy, or risk, immediately shift your thinking toward responsible AI principles.
Is it practical?	Sometimes organizations want to solve every problem with AI. An AI transformation leader understands that not every process requires AI. You should always consider cost, complexity, user adoption, and operational impact.	In the exam, the best answer is often the solution that delivers meaningful value with reasonable effort and risk.
Can the organization adopt It?	A technically perfect solution can still fail if people refuse to use it. Adoption is one of the most important concepts in the exam. Always consider user training, executive sponsorship, a communication plan, and AI Champions.	Remember that successful transformation is never only about technology. It is about people.

Sample questions and how to use them

The sample questions in this appendix were crafted to ensure that you understand how to think through the question, not because you'll see these same questions on the exam. The goal is to ensure that you are rationalizing the question using the right approach. With that in mind, let's get started!

Question 1

A company wants employees to spend less time searching for information through emails, documents, and meetings. What should the organization prioritize?

A. Building a custom AI model

B. Increasing cloud storage

C. Implementing Microsoft 365 Copilot

D. Purchasing more laptops

2 Revisit the Microsoft responsible AI principles at *https://www.microsoft.com/en-us/ai/principles-and-approach.*

Before answering the question, ask yourself: What is the business problem? In this case, it is that employees waste time finding information. Now, ask yourself: From the given options, which solution directly improves productivity and information retrieval? You will easily conclude that the answer is C (Microsoft 365 Copilot).

Question 2

A company discovers that its AI solution occasionally produces inaccurate information. What should leadership focus on first?

A. Expanding deployment

B. Increasing model size

C. Evaluating reliability and governance

D. Purchasing more licenses

In this case, the first thing you must understand is that this question is about responsible AI. The key phrase is *inaccurate information*. That points directly to reliability, which means C is the answer. If you allow your technical side to speak louder, you may overthink and start creating hypotheses that may lead you to the wrong conclusion.

Question 3

A company wants employees to adopt AI tools faster. What should leadership prioritize?

A. More technical features

B. Larger language models

C. AI Champions and training

D. More storage capacity

Let's start by saying that this is an adoption question. Whenever you see adoption, think: people, training, change management, and AI Champions. In this case, the correct answer is C.

Question 4

An organization wants to justify its AI investment. What metric should leaders focus on?

A. Number of prompts

B. Number of licenses

C. Business outcomes and ROI

D. Number of models deployed

Remember that this exam focuses heavily on value, and business leaders care about outcomes, which leads to letter C as the correct answer.

Final thoughts

When you sit down to take the AB-731 exam, I want you to keep one thing in mind: you are not getting evaluated as a developer, an engineer, or a data scientist. You don't need to think about writing code, training models, or designing technical architecture. Instead, put yourself in the shoes of an AI transformation leader. Imagine you're sitting in a meeting with business executives trying to solve real organizational challenges.

As you read each question, ask yourself: Where is the business value? How will people adopt this solution? What governance or responsible AI considerations should be taken into account? What outcome is the organization trying to achieve? The exam is much less about technology and much more about leadership, strategy, and business impact. If you approach every question through that lens, you'll find that many of the answers become much clearer. Also, when multiple answers seem correct, prioritize the one that:

- Creates business value.
- Aligns with responsible AI principles.
- Improves adoption.
- Supports organizational goals.
- Minimizes risk.

If it helps, Figure A-2 has a visual representation of how you should approach questions where multiple answers seem to be correct:

FIGURE A-2 Mindset for the exam

In Figure A-2, the best answer is B: Build a solution that is explainable, easy to use, and solves a high-impact problem. Here is the breakdown of why this is the best answer:

- **Creates business value:** It solves a high-impact business problem rather than focusing only on technical excellence.
- **Aligns with responsible AI principles:** An explainable solution supports transparency and accountability, which are core responsible AI principles.
- **Improves adoption:** If users can understand and easily use the solution; they are much more likely to trust and adopt it.
- **Supports organizational goals:** The focus is on solving a business problem, which directly aligns with organizational objectives.
- **Minimizes risk:** Explainable and well-understood systems are generally easier to govern, audit, and troubleshoot.

You may ask, why are the others less appropriate? Let's review them:

- **Option A: Build the most accurate model, even if it's complex and hard to explain:** This prioritizes technical performance over explainability, adoption, and governance. Many AI transformation leader questions are designed to tempt you into choosing the most technically advanced option.
- **Option C: Build a solution using the newest model, even if it's not well-tested:** This introduces unnecessary risk and conflicts with responsible AI and governance principles.
- **Option D: Build a solution that requires minimal change to existing processes:** While this may help with adoption, it doesn't necessarily maximize business value or solve the most important problem.

Now that you have reached the end of this book, I hope you walk away with more than just knowledge about AI. My goal was to help you understand how to create meaningful impact with AI by focusing on business value, driving positive outcomes, and doing so in a secure, responsible, and sustainable way. If you embrace the mindset of an AI transformation leader, you will start looking beyond the technology itself and focus on how AI can solve real business challenges, empower people, and support organizational goals. Passing the exam will simply be the natural result of the effort and preparation you put into your studies. Remember, this exam does not test your ability to think like an engineer or a developer; it tests your ability to think like a leader. Trust the process, study consistently, and avoid overthinking every question. Most importantly, enjoy the learning journey. I wish you the very best of luck on your exam and on your journey as an AI transformation leader.

Index

Numerics

70–20-10 development philosophy, 57

A

AB-731, 97–98, 103–104
  pillar questions, 101
  preparation, 100–101
  sample questions, 101–102
  topics, 98–99
accountability, 51
Agentic AI. *See also* AI agents; Microsoft Copilot Studio
  autonomy, 2
  delegated trust, 92–93
AI adoption, 68–69. *See also* AI strategy
  barriers, 58–59
    adoption gap from pilot to scale, 60
    cost and ROI uncertainty, 60
    data quality, 60
    human resistance, 59
    lack of expertise, 59
    leadership perception versus employee's reality, 59
    organizational silos and lack of strategy, 60
    security, 79
  build-buy-extend framework, 38–39
  establish an adoption team, 56–58
  plan for adoption across the organization, 56
  planning, 56
AI agents
  attack vectors, 92
  behavior-based user and sign-in risk scoring, 77
  conditional access, 77–78
  DSPM (data security posture management), 79–81
  identity, 71, 72
  information protection, 82–85
  risky, 76
  security risks, 71
  trust boundaries, 84
AI council, 54–56, 68
AI strategy, 58–59
  establish an adoption team, 56–58
  establish an AI Champions program, 60–61
    align champions with real business outcomes, 62–63
    create a feedback loop, 62
    define the role clearly, 61–62
    establish the right mindset, 61
    provide structured enablement, 62
    recognition and awards, 62
    scale the program thoughtfully, 63
  establish an AI council to guide oversight and cross-functional alignment, 54–56
  governance, 53–54
  plan for AI adoption across the organization, 56
  Responsible AI alignment, 49–50
  trust, 49
AI transformation, 1
AI Transformation Leader Exam. *See* AB-731
AI-driven hiring discrimination, 49
algorithms, 3
Analyst, use cases, 37–38
augmentation, Gen AI, 11–12
automation, Gen AI, 11–12
autonomy, AI agents, 2
Azure AI Search, 42
Azure Machine Learning, 12
Azure OpenAI, 12
Azure Vision, 42

B

barriers to AI adoption
  adoption gap from pilot to scale, 60
  cost and ROI uncertainty, 60
  data quality, 60
  human resistance, 59
  lack of expertise, 59
  leadership perception versus employee's reality, 59
  organizational silos and lack of strategy, 60
behavior-based risk scoring, 77
bias, AI models, 10

business processes
mapping to Copilot, 24–25
mapping to Microsoft AI Solutions, 35–36
mapping to Microsoft Foundry services, 40–41

C

capabilities
Microsoft 365 Copilot, 28–30
Microsoft 365 Copilot Chat, 27–28
Microsoft Copilot Studio, 30–32
Microsoft Foundry, 39–40
Microsoft Graph, 32–33
case law
Equal Employment Opportunity Commission (EEOC) v. iTutorGroup (2023), 49
Mata v. Avianca, 9
chain-of-thought prompting, 14
cloud security
risk prioritization and contextual security recommendations, 88–90
threat protection for AI workloads, 90–94
compliance, regulatory, 50
conditional access, AI agents, 77–78
consumption-based model, 7, 8
contextual grounding within the prompt, 13
Copilot, 26–27. *See also* Microsoft 365 Copilot; Microsoft Copilot
context awareness, 27
differences in capabilities between versions, 26–27
licensing, 63–64, 65–66
layered approach, 64
monthly model, 64, 65
pay-as-you-go models, 64, 65
map business process and use-cases, 24–25
Researcher, 36–37
Copilot Studio, 5, 12
copilots, 1
cost models, Gen AI, 7

D

data exposure, 34
data governance for AI, 85–87
data protection, 79
data quality, 17–18
deep learning, 2, 3
documentation, AI governance policies, 54
DSPM (data security posture management), 79–81

E-F

ethics, AI-driven hiring discrimination, 49. *See also* Responsible AI

fabricated content, 9–10
facial recognition, bias, 10
fairness, 51
few-shot prompting, 13–14
fine-tuned models, 6, 7

G

Gen AI, 2, 3
adoption, 1
augmentation, 11–12
automation, 11–12
benefits of Microsoft Foundry services, 44–46
bias, 10
choosing a solution, 4
direct costs, 7–8
infrastructure and integration costs, 8–9
ROI, 8–9
security and compliance, 5
use cases, 5
consumption-based model, 7–8
cost models, 7
data integration, 4
data quality, 17–18
differences with traditional AI, 3–4
discriminatory practices, 49
fabricated content, 9–10
fine-tuned models, 6, 7
fully customized models, 4
grounding, 15–16
overreliance, 10
platform-based approaches, 4
prebuilt solutions, 4
pretrained models, 6, 7
prompt engineering, 13
chain-of-thought prompting, 14
constraints, 14
contextual grounding within the prompt, 13
few-shot prompting, 13–14
output structuring, 14
role prompting, 13
RAG (retrieval-augmented generation), 16–17
reliability, 10
unstructured data, 17
value, 11–12

governance, 1, 2
AI, 53–54, 68
data, 85–87
integrated Microsoft AI solution, 34–35
grounding, 15–16, 27–28

H-I

hallucination, 9–10

identity. *See also* Microsoft Entra
AI agents, 71, 72
signals, 74–75
inclusiveness, 51
information protection, 82–83
governance integration, 84–85
operating philosophy, 84
protection granularity, 84
protection of AI-generated content, 84
trust boundaries for AI agents, 84
use cases, 83
integrated Microsoft AI solution, 33–34
data exposure, 34
governance, 34–35
operational visibility, 35
prompt and response safety, 34
trust, 35

J-K-L

licensing
Copilot, 26–27, 63–64, 65–66
layered approach, 64
monthly model, 64, 65
pay-as-you-go models, 64, 65
Microsoft 365 Copilot, 27
Microsoft Foundry, 66
pay-as-you-go models, 67
PTUs, 67, 68
LLMs (large language models), 2–3

M

machine learning
deep learning, 3
solution lifecycle, 19–20
use cases, 19
Microsoft 365 Copilot, 5, 9, 12
contextual responses, 23–24
licensing, 27, 65
Outlook and Teams, 29–30
use cases, 27
Word and PowerPoint, 29
Microsoft 365 Copilot Chat, 12, 27–28
Microsoft AI Solutions
build-buy-extend framework, 38–39
business process mapping, 35–36
Microsoft Copilot, 5
integrated AI, 24
use cases, 26
Microsoft Copilot Studio
building AI agents, decision matrix, 32
capabilities, 30–32
use cases, 27
Microsoft Defender for Cloud, 87
AI-SPM (AI Security Posture Management), 87–88, 89–90
DCSPM (Defender Cloud Security Posture Management), 88
Defender for AI Services, 92
risk prioritization and contextual security recommendations, 88–90
threat protection for AI workloads, 90–94
Microsoft Entra, 71
adaptive access with conditional access, 77–78
Agent ID, 72–74
Agent ID dashboard, 73–74
behavior-based user and sign in risk scoring, 77
ID Protection, 75–76, 77
identity signals, 74–75
Microsoft Foundry, 4, 5, 12
Azure AI Search, 42
Azure AI Search + Azure OpenAI, 12
Azure Vision, 42
business process mapping, 40–41
capabilities, 39–40
licensing, 66
pay-as-you-go models, 67
PTUs, 67, 68
RAG architecture, 12
Responsible AI support, 45
scalability, 44, 45–46
security, 44, 45–46
Microsoft Graph, 24, 32–33
Microsoft Purview
data classification and sensitive data detection, 81–82
data governance for AI, 85–87

data protection, 79
DSPM (data security posture management), 79–81
information protection
governance integration, 84–85
operating philosophy, 84
protection granularity, 84
protection of AI-generated content, 84
trust boundaries for AI agents, 84
information protection for AI apps and agents, 82–85
machine learning classifiers, 82
SITs (Sensitive Information Types), 82
Microsoft Responsible AI, 10–11
Microsoft Security Copilot, 12, 27
models
comparison, 7
fine-tuned, 6
matching to a business need, 43–44
pretrained, 6
monthly subscriptions, Copilot, 64, 65

N-O

neural networks, 2, 3
NLP (natural language processing), 3

operational visibility, integrated Microsoft AI solution, 35
output structuring, 14
overreliance, 10
oversight, AI council, 54–56

P

pay-as-you-go models
Copilot, 64, 65
Microsoft Foundry, 67
policies
AI governance, 54
conditional access, 77–78
predictive forecasting, 5
pretrained models, 6, 7
principles
governance, 53
Responsible AI, 51–52
privacy, Rep, 51
prompt engineering, 8, 13
chain-of-thought prompting, 14
constraints, 14
contextual grounding within the prompt, 13
few-shot prompting, 13–14
output structuring, 14
role prompting, 13
PTUs (provisioned throughput units), 67, 68

Q-R

RAG (retrieval-augmented generation), 4, 5, 8, 12, 16–17
regulatory compliance, 50
reliability
Gen AI, 10
Responsible AI, 51
Researcher, use cases, 36–38
Responsible AI, 5, 10–11, 45–46, 68
accountability, 51
aligning with AI strategy, 49–50
fairness, 51
goals, 52
inclusiveness, 51
layered approach, 52
Microsoft Foundry, 45
privacy and security, 51
regulatory compliance, 50
reliability and safety, 51
risk assessment and mitigation, 50
transparency, 51
risk scoring, 77
risky sign-in, 76
ROI (return on investment), Gen AI, 8–9
role prompting, 13
roles and responsibilities
AI adoption team, 57–58
AI Champions, 61–62
AI council, 55–56

S

scalability, Microsoft Foundry, 44, 45–46
security
cloud, risk prioritization and contextual security recommendations, 88–90
data classification and sensitive data detection in AI, 81–82
data protection, 79
DSPM (data security posture management), 79–81
identity
AI agents, 71, 72
signals, 74–75

information protection
governance integration, 84–85
operating philosophy, 84
protection granularity, 84
protection of AI-generated content, 84
trust boundaries for AI agents, 84
use cases, 83
information protection for AI apps and agents, 82–83
Microsoft Foundry, 44, 45–46
Responsible AI, 51
risk scoring, 76
Zero Trust, 72, 74
signals, identity, 74–75
sign-in, behavior-based risk scoring, 77

T

tokens, 8
traditional AI, differences with Gen AI, 3–4
training, 70-20-10 approach, 57
transparency, 51
trust, 35, 49

U-V

unstructured data, 17
use cases. *See also* business processes; capabilities
Analyst, 37–38
Copilot, 24–25
Gen AI, 5
information protection, 83
machine learning, 19
Microsoft 365 Copilot, 27
Microsoft Copilot, 26
Microsoft Copilot Studio, 27
Microsoft Foundry, 40–41
Microsoft Security Copilot, 27
Researcher, 36–38
users, behavior-based risk scoring, 77

value, Gen AI, 11–12

W-X-Y-Z

Zero Trust, 72, 74. *See also* trust